LIFE
EXPLORES
The Bible
50 MOST IMPORTANT PEOPLE

Paolo Veronese's *Last Supper* (16th century) shows Jesus blessing an apostle.

CONTENTS

1. IN THE BEGINNING

2. THE NATION OF ISRAEL

3. JESUS AND HIS DISCIPLES

4. THE ACTS OF THE APOSTLES

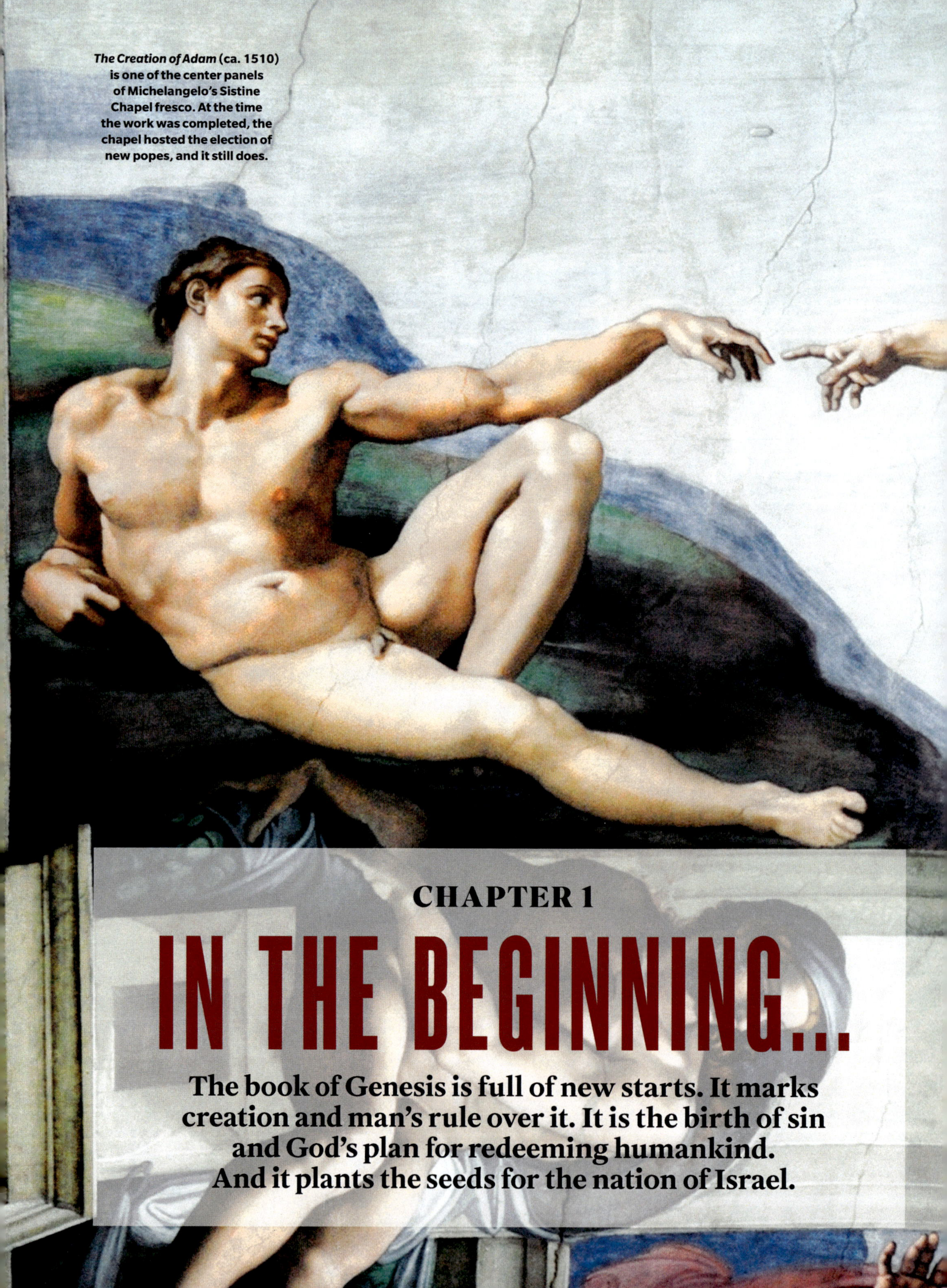

The Creation of Adam (ca. 1510) is one of the center panels of Michelangelo's Sistine Chapel fresco. At the time the work was completed, the chapel hosted the election of new popes, and it still does.

CHAPTER 1

IN THE BEGINNING...

The book of Genesis is full of new starts. It marks creation and man's rule over it. It is the birth of sin and God's plan for redeeming humankind. And it plants the seeds for the nation of Israel.

Jan Brueghel the Elder foreshadows the fall of Adam and Eve in the background of *The Temptation in the Garden of Eden* (ca. 1600).

GENESIS 2, 3

Adam and Eve: The First Man and Woman

The first humans learn that knowledge comes at a price.

The second chapter of Genesis opens with a description of a bare earth. There is no vegetation, no rain, and no one to till the ground. God then plants an earthly paradise called Eden. He creates a human body out of dust and breathes life into it. Adam, the first human, is created.

All is not paradise in the Garden of Eden. God notices that man is alone and states that this is not good. According to the story, God brings creatures to Adam so that Adam can give each of them a name—which he does. When Adam finishes naming all the animals, God notes that none are identified as man's helper. So he sends Adam to sleep, removes a rib, and creates a woman from it. He then presents her to Adam, who promptly identifies her as woman, "for out of man this one was taken." (Genesis 2:23) The woman is not called Eve until the next chapter.

The innocence of the first man and woman is emphasized by the statement that they were both naked and not embarrassed by their nakedness. This has practical and theological significance in the next chapter.

THE FALL FROM GRACE

What was life like in the Garden of Eden before the Fall and how long did it last? Curiously, the Hebrew Bible is silent on this topic. Much of what is believed about life in Eden is presumed from what Adam and Eve lost in the Fall.

The narrative goes directly from the creation of the first couple to the commission of original sin.

The stage had been set for a conflict by God's declaration: "You may freely eat of every tree of the garden; but of the tree of the knowledge of good and evil you shall not eat, for in the day that you eat of it you shall die." (Genesis 2:16-17)

Chapter 3 opens with a new character, the serpent. The Hebrew Bible offers no description other than to say the snake was craftier than any other wild animal.

The serpent begins conversing with the woman by asking if God has specifically forbidden the man and the woman from eating from any tree in the garden.

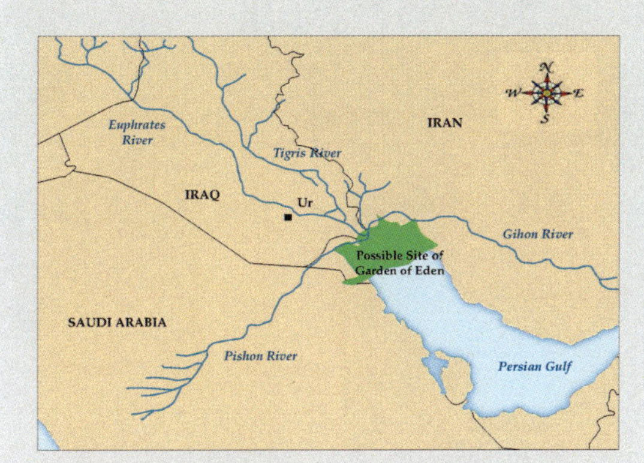

WHERE WAS THE GARDEN OF EDEN?
The description in Genesis 2:10-14 situates the Garden of Eden at the headwaters of the Pishon, the Gihon, the Tigris, and the Euphrates Rivers. While the Tigris and the Euphrates still flow, the Pishon and Gihon have yet to be located definitively, and maps that show them, such as the one above, are speculative. It is possible that Eden was located near Babylon and Ur, both of which are in Mesopotamia, or in modern-day Iraq.

When Eve responds that she and the man will die if they sample fruit from the tree, the snake goads her on: "You will not die; for God knows that when you eat of it your eyes will be opened, and you will be like God."

The serpent then contradicts what God has said and suggests that the command is part of a hidden agenda to deny Adam and Eve knowledge that has been reserved for God.

Since the fruit is appealing as food, delightful to look at, and has the added benefit of conferring wisdom, Eve eats it and gives it to Adam to taste as well. Immediately Adam's and Eve's eyes are opened.

THE FIRST CLOTHES

The first thing Adam and Eve focus on is their nakedness. Embarrassed, they sew fig leaves together to make clothes.

Later that day, when God is strolling in the garden, Adam and Eve conceal themselves. When God calls out to them, they say they are hiding because they are afraid of their nakedness.

God asks the humans who told them they were naked and accuses Adam and Eve of eating the fruit from the forbidden tree.

ADAM SHIFTS THE BLAME

Adam tries to shift the blame by saying it was the woman who gave him the fruit. Eve, in turn, implicates the serpent, explaining that it tricked her into tasting the fruit. God then turns to the serpent and places a curse on it.

God returns to Eve and curses her with pains in childbirth and submission to her husband. God tells Adam that because he followed Eve into sin, he has to work hard to make anything grow.

God also curses humans with death, saying, "You are dust." (Genesis 3:19)

The Temptation **(1899) by William Strang repeats a common misconception that Genesis identifies the forbidden fruit as an apple.**

The Italian painter Tiziano Vecelli, known as Titian, shows the beginning of human violence in *Cain and Abel* (ca. 1543).

GENESIS 4

Cain and Abel: Siblings at War

Genesis reveals that human conflict is as old as mankind.

The theme of alienation and loss that begins with the story of the Fall continues with Cain and Abel. Cain, the firstborn son of Eve, follows in his father's footsteps as a farmer. Abel, his younger brother, becomes a herdsman.

As the young men reach adulthood, both worship God by offering sacrifices. God receives Abel's offering from his flock. Cain's offering of produce or grain, however, is not well regarded.

Though God assures Cain that he will accept his offering if he does well, Cain is so jealous of Abel that he murders him.

When God confronts Cain and asks where Abel has gone, Cain famously replies, "Am I my brother's keeper?" (Genesis 4:9) God sentences Cain to wander the earth, a punishment Cain fears will make others want to kill him.

To ensure his safety, God places a mark on Cain, which serves as a warning that anyone who murders Cain will suffer God's wrath.

The story of Cain and Abel sets the tone for much of what follows in the Hebrew Bible. The world is divided into "us" and "them." However, instead of rooting the seeds of rivalry in selfish ambition, the story of Cain and Abel involves God in the conflict. It is God's favor that they both seek, and it is God who advises Cain to try harder.

GENESIS 6, 9

Noah: Builder of the Ark

God finds a righteous man to restart the human race and all of creation.

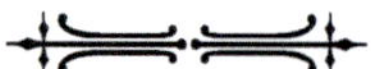

The flood narrative in Genesis 6–9, commonly referred to as the story of Noah's ark, highlights God's goodness. While the rest of creation has become so wicked that it cannot be redeemed, God, in order to show mercy, chooses Noah to rescue not only the human race but all of creation. The account also reveals a dark and troubling element: God makes arrangements for Noah and his family to be saved, but the rest of humanity perishes.

God gives Noah specific instructions for building an ark to preserve his family and a male and female of every land animal on earth. Noah obeys and spends 100 years building the ark. Then when the rains begin, he gathers his family and the animals into the ark.

The torrential downpour lasts 40 days and 40 nights and floods the earth.

A PROMISE FROM GOD

After 150 days, the waters recede enough for the ark to land in the Ararat Mountains, in what is now modern-day Turkey. It is another 40 days before Noah is able to open a window, and the first thing he does is send out a series of birds to see if they can locate dry land.

When a dove returns to the ark with an olive branch in its mouth, Noah knows the waters have dried up enough that the ark's journey will soon be over.

After Noah determines that it is safe, he releases all of the animals.

The first thing Noah and his sons do is build an altar and send up offerings to God, who is pleased. God, in return, promises never to flood the entire earth again. As a sign of his promise, God puts a rainbow in the sky.

Fresco of Raphael's *Noah Building the Ark* (1483–1520) in St. Peter's Basilica, Vatican City.

GENESIS 12

Abraham: The Father of Many Nations

God affirms his covenant with humanity and identifies the Promised Land.

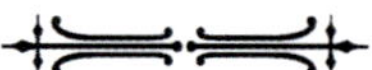

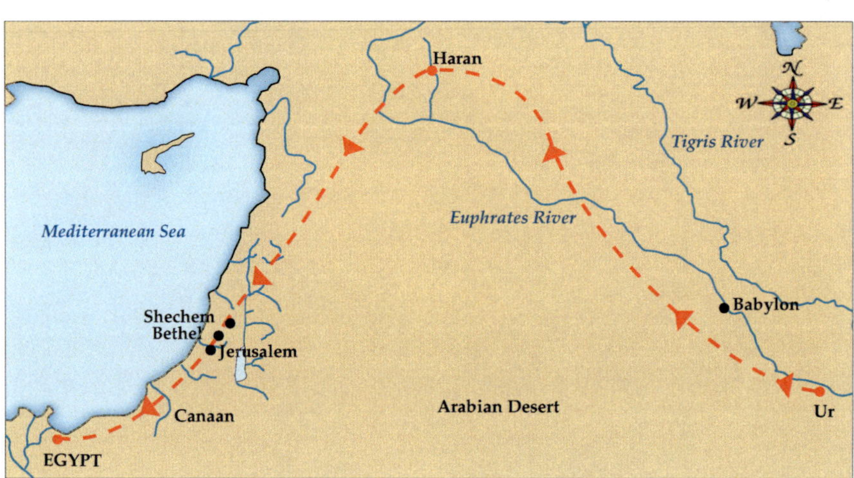

Beginning with Genesis 12, the Bible's narrative moves from the world at large to the members of a single family. Here is the story of Abram, later to become Abraham, and his line of descendants.

This chapter begins with a call and a promise from God to Abram, who is from Ur of the Chaldees. God's pledge consists of three parts:

- **A land.** Abram is to leave his homeland and family and journey to a land that God will reveal to him.
- **A people.** God will make Abram a great name, and he will father a great nation to be a great blessing.
- **A blessing.** Those who bless Abram will be blessed, and those who curse him will be cursed, and through Abram all the nations of the earth will receive a blessing.

Abram leaves the town of Haran, where he is living, and with his wife Sarai, nephew Lot, and many relatives, he journeys south to Canaan.

As Abram reaches the ancient city of Shechem (near the modern-day West Bank town of Nablus), God identifies land that Abram's descendants will possess. Abram begins to build altars and offers sacrifices at strategic locations. Each altar represents a claim he is staking to the land for his posterity.

ABRAM'S FAMILY

The story of Abram's family moves quickly to establish the passing of generations: Ishmael, Abram's first son, is ultimately banished to the wilderness with his mother, Hagar. Isaac, Abram's son with Sarah, produces two boys. These sons are named Jacob and Esau, and each son fathers a dozen male offspring of his own. Genesis first focuses on Jacob, who also has 12 sons, and then on Joseph, the second youngest and favorite son of Jacob.

In this telling, Abram's numerous male descendants are not a cohesive lot. The family members often are at odds with one another, and they rarely establish close relationships. In fact, a common story thread found in Genesis and throughout the Bible is the internecine strife among close relatives—a dynamic that is foreshadowed early on with the brother-versus-brother tale of Cain and Abel.

Abram on His Journey to Canaan by Gustave Doré (19th century). Opposite: The map traces Abram's journey from Ur up to Haran, then down to Canaan, and eventually to Egypt.

VERSES AND INSIGHTS

How Abraham is connected to three faiths, and where to find his hometown today

ABRAHAM: THE GREAT INFLUENCER

The story of Abraham is significant because it is deeply embedded in three important faith traditions. Islam connects its heritage to Abraham's first son, Ishmael, and his descendants. Judaism traces its patrimony through Abraham's second son, Isaac. Christianity, while not claiming a biological connection to Abraham, does profess to be spiritually linked to his faith, particularly as it is expressed by his blood descendant, Jesus of Nazareth.

WHERE WAS UR?

Genesis identifies the city of Ur, also called Ur Kasdim, as Abraham's birthplace. Some have questioned if Ur was an actual city. Today, many scholars believe that the ruins of a massive temple complex near Nasiriyah, Iraq, mark the site of the ancient Sumerian city of Ur.

GENESIS 16, 18

Sarah: The Mother of Isaac

Abraham's faithful wife comes up with a plan to give him descendants.

Years pass, but Sarai does not conceive a child. She knows that for God's promise to be fulfilled and for Abram to father a great nation, her husband must produce an heir.

Sarai comes up with a plan: She persuades Abram to father a child with her young Egyptian slave, Hagar. The arrangement permits Sarai to keep her status as family matriarch and provides Abram a son through a surrogate.

Yet as Hagar's pregnancy progresses, the slave becomes increasingly contemptuous of Sarai. In turn, Sarai is so abusive toward Hagar that she flees to the wilderness. There, Hagar is found by an angel who persuades her to return and to submit to Sarai's authority. The angel promises Hagar that he will greatly multiply her offspring, but he warns that there will be perpetual strife between her son and all his kin. Hagar goes back to Sarai and gives birth to Ishmael, whose name means "God has hearkened," in reference to God having heard her cries in the wilderness.

Thirteen years pass and Abram is now 99 years old. God appears to him again, this time in person, to renew his earlier promise that Abram will father a nation. God changes Abram's name to Abraham and Sarai's name to Sarah. He then says he will give the land of Canaan as a perpetual inheritance for Abraham's descendants.

Genesis 18 begins some time later with the appearance of three men whom Abraham perceives to be divine. The visitors reiterate God's promise that Sarah will soon bear a son. Sarah, overhearing their conversation, laughs at the idea since she is now advanced in years and unlikely to conceive. The visitors remark on Sarah laughing at the promise, although she denies it.

Hagar Introduced to Abraham **by Victor Orsel (19th century).**

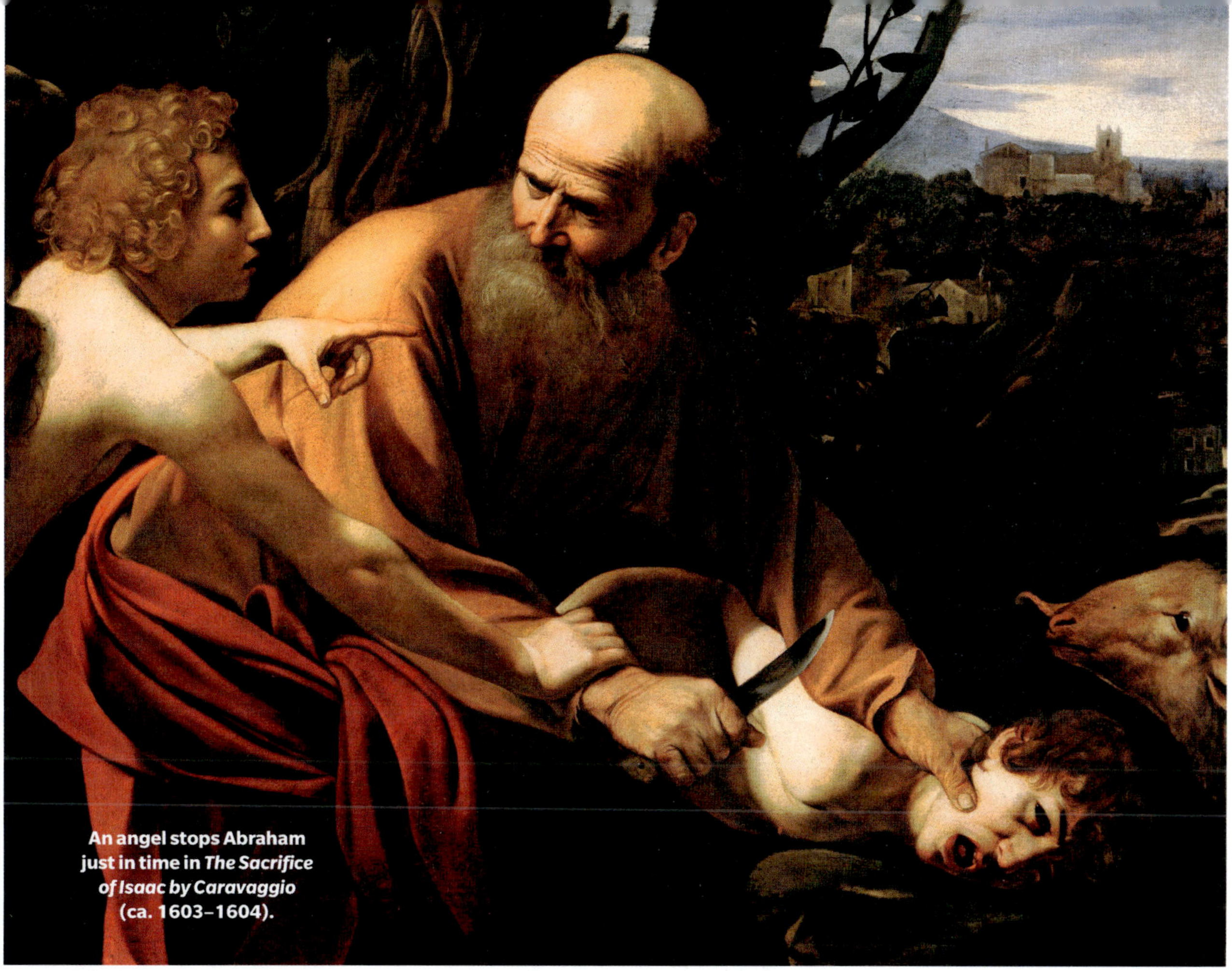

An angel stops Abraham just in time in *The Sacrifice of Isaac* by *Caravaggio* (ca. 1603–1604).

GENESIS 21, 22

Isaac: Abraham's Long-Awaited Son

Sarah finally conceives a child for her husband.

As God has promised, Sarah, who is 90, gives birth to a son and she names him Isaac, meaning "laughter." To protect Isaac's inheritance from Hagar's son, Ishmael, Sarah insists that Abraham send mother and son away. Abraham is reluctant. He loves Ishmael and agrees to banish his firstborn only after an angel promises that Ishmael also will be the father of a great nation. Ishmael goes on to father 12 sons, from whom would come 12 tribal nations. Hagar gets lost in the wilderness but then is rescued from starvation by an angel.

The worst is not over for Abraham, who must now face the most severe test of his faith and willingness to obey all of God's commands. God instructs the aging patriarch to take Isaac, his promised heir, and to sacrifice him on the top of Mount Moriah. Abraham, with his mature faith in God, sets out with his son to comply. When Isaac asks why they have made all the necessary preparations for a sacrifice but have no animal to offer, Abraham replies, "God himself will provide the lamb for a burnt offering, my son." (Genesis 22:8)

The narrative describes Abraham building the altar, ordering the wood on it, and then placing Isaac atop the pile. However, just as Abraham is about to plunge his knife into the boy's body, an angel stops his hand, and God points to a ram that is caught in the thicket of nearby bushes. The father and son are able to make a sacrifice of the ram.

Italian painter Gregorio Lazzarini shows Isaac's future wife meeting Abraham's servant Eliezer in *Rebecca and Eliezer* (ca. 1705).

GENESIS 24

Rebekah: Isaac's Bride

Abraham sends his son to their homeland to find a wife.

When Isaac is 37, Sarah passes away and Abraham decides it is time for Isaac to marry. He sends his servant to their ancestral homeland to find a member of the family for his son Isaac to take as a bride.

The caravan heads north and arrives at a well. One of Abraham's servants, hesitant to trust his own judgment, asks God for help. He requests that the first woman who offers to provide water for him and his 10 camels would be Isaac's bride. While the servant is praying, a young woman shows up at the well and draws a jar of water. The servant asks her for a drink, and she readily offers her jar to him. The woman then suggests she also can give water to his camels until their thirst is satisfied, and she returns to the well to refill her water jar.

The servant is delighted with such an obvious answer to his prayer and inquires about the woman's parentage. He discovers she is indeed a close relative of Abraham, and he offers her a gold nose ring and gold bracelets. He asks to be taken to meet her father, and the young woman, named Rebekah, agrees.

On the way home, Rebekah encounters her brother Laban, who notices the new jewelry she is wearing. Rebekah shares her story, and Laban immediately ushers the servant and the rest of Abraham's caravan to their camp so they can clean up from their journey, rest, and eat.

The servant explains that the group is on a mission to find a wife for Isaac and that Rebekah is the answer to his prayer at the well. He then asks if Laban is willing to proceed with marriage arrangements for his sister right away.

Laban agrees, and the caravan returns to Canaan with Rebekah. Isaac marries Rebekah and is comforted after his mother's death.

VERSES AND INSIGHTS

Behind a name change, and why it makes sense that the search for Isaac's wife starts at a well

NEW DESTINIES

Some scholars believe that Abram and Sarai's names change to Abraham and Sarah because of the couple's new destinies. Abram, which means"exalted father," becomes Abraham, "father of many nations." He now is the patriarch of a new people in a new land, fulfilling God's promise: "I will make you a great nation." Likewise, in changing Sarai ("my princess") to Sarah ("the princess"), God is making good on a pledge that Sarai will be the mother of millions "and kings shall come from you."

VERSE TO KNOW

"Shall I indeed bear a child, now that I am old?" (Gen. 18:13)

AT THE WELL

In pastoral cultures, wells were meeting places where shepherds exchanged news with travelers and women congregated to draw water, so it is logical that the search for Isaac's wife starts at a watering hole.

GENESIS 25, 27

Jacob and Esau: Rival Brothers

God tells Rebekah that her younger son will supplant his older twin brother.

Like Sarah, Rebekah remains childless for many years of marriage. She finally conceives twins after Isaac prays on her behalf, but the babies struggle with each other even in the womb. Rebekah asks God why this is, and he explains that she has two nations inside of her fighting for dominance and that the elder will serve the younger.

This notion carries over into the names of the boys when they are born. The elder son, who is red and covered with hair, is dubbed Esau, or "hairy." The younger son, who grips the heel of his older brother as he enters the world, is named Jacob, which translates as "supplanter."

Genesis summarizes Esau's character in an episode in which he returns empty-handed from a hunting expedition. Famished, Esau comes upon Jacob cooking a pot of stew and asks to eat. Jacob agrees, but only if Esau will hand over his birthright. Esau agrees, selling his birthright for a bowl of stew.

Years later when Isaac lies dying, Jacob tricks Esau again, this time with Rebekah's help. Mother and son convince Isaac, who is now blind, that the person serving him his final meal is Esau when it is really Jacob. Isaac unwittingly confers his blessing on Jacob, the younger son, making him the family patriarch. He utters: "Be lord over your brothers, and may your mother's sons bow down to you. Cursed be everyone who curses you, and blessed be everyone who blesses you." (Genesis 27:29)

Esau also gets a blessing from Isaac, but he is now so filled with hatred for his brother that he plots to murder him. As Isaac lies dying in Canaan, he instructs Jacob to return to Haran, the family's ancestral homeland, to find a wife, removing Jacob from Esau's murderous reach.

Italian Baroque painter Bernardo Strozzi portrays Jacob tricking his father in *Isaac Blessing Jacob* (ca. 1625).

GENESIS 28, 33

Jacob: Prince of God

Isaac's son seeks to marry Rachel and ends up with two wives.

On the way back to his homeland, Jacob stops to sleep and dreams of angels climbing a ladder to heaven. God speaks to Jacob, reaffirming the gift of land he promised Abraham and Isaac. Upon awaking, Jacob names the spot Bethel ("House of God") and vows that if God protects him on his journey, he will take God as his Lord and will give a tenth of all that he earns.

When Jacob arrives in the territory of his ancestors, he visits a well and asks if any of the shepherds know of Laban in Haran. Laban is Jacob's uncle, the brother of Rebekah. Just then, Laban's beautiful daughter Rachel

In *Jacob Meets Rachel* (1836), Austrian painter Joseph von Führich portrays the couple's first encounter. Opposite: *Jacob Wrestles with an Angel* by Edward Jakob von Steinle (19th century).

arrives with a flock of sheep. Jacob rolls away the stone covering the well, waters her flock, and announces that he is Rebekah's son. Rachel runs to tell her father, who greets Jacob warmly, houses him, and gives him work for a month. Asked by Laban what he wants in compensation, Jacob says to marry Rachel. The men agree that after seven years of labor, Jacob will take Rachel as his wife, and at the end of the period, Laban hosts a huge wedding However, instead of presenting Jacob with Rachel on their wedding night, he substitutes her older sister, Leah. When Jacob confronts Laban, he says it is not customary for the younger sister to marry first and offers to give Rachel to Jacob after another seven years of labor, and Jacob assents.

Six years later, Jacob is so rich, he fears that Laban's field hands are jealous and leaves Haran, taking Rachel and Leah with him. Infuriated, Laban pursues his son-in-law, who struggles with what to do. In his sleep, Jacob meets an angel sent by God; they wrestle, and when the angel gains the upper hand, Jacob says he will let go only if the angel blesses him. The angel agrees, renaming Jacob Israel ("Prince of God"). Jacob continues to Canaan to find Esau. Coming face to face, the brothers embrace and weep.

Joseph's brothers show Jacob the coat of many colors to prove that Joseph is dead in this work by an unknown artist (1855).

GENESIS 37, 38–49

Joseph: From a Slave to an Egyptian Official

Jacob's son faces slavery and imprisonment, rises to power under Pharaoh, and eventually reconciles with his family.

Between his two wives and two concubines, Jacob now has 11 sons, but they are so unruly and hateful that Jacob is forced to move the family from Shechem south to Bethel.

He continues a semi-nomadic existence for years, moving often. During one such transfer, Rachel, Jacob's favorite wife, dies while giving birth to their youngest son, named Benjamin.

Because Jacob loved Rachel dearly, he treats Joseph, the second-youngest son, the best. He designs a special coat for him as a sign of his approval, alienating his other sons. Joseph creates even more conflict by relating symbolic dreams that suggest his brothers will bow down to him. The brothers consider Joseph ambitious and a potential threat and plot to kill him.

They first agree to slay Joseph when he comes searching for them out in the fields with the livestock. But the oldest brother, Reuben, persuades his siblings to instead sell Joseph into slavery and to make it look like an accidental death.

The 11 brothers strip Joseph of his robe and toss him into a pit. Then they rip the garment into pieces, cover it in blood, and present it to their father. Joseph is discovered by nomadic merchants, who sell him as a slave to men in a caravan headed south to Egypt. The brothers don't know the fate of their sibling.

JOSEPH INTERPRETS PHAROAH'S DREAMS

In Egypt, Joseph is sold into the household of Potiphar, an officer in Pharaoh's guard. Joseph advances within the household but is thrown into prison after Potiphar's wife unfairly accuses him of attempting to violate her.

Joseph begins interpreting the dreams of two fellow inmates, Pharaoh's ex–chief baker and ex–chief cupbearer, and becomes a valued figure in the prison. The men agree to mention Joseph to Pharaoh after they are released. However, when the cupbearer gets his job back, he forgets about Joseph. It is only two years later, when Pharaoh has some bad dreams, that Joseph is summoned and hears what Pharaoh has seen at night.

In the first dream, Pharaoh is standing by the Nile when seven fat cows come out of the water and begin eating the grass along the riverbank. Then, seven thin cows come out of the river and eat the fat cows, but even after devouring them, the thin cows remain thin.

In the second dream, Pharaoh sees seven fat ears of grain growing on a stalk, waving in the wind. Then, seven

Joseph of Egypt in Prison by German Bohemian painter Anton Raphael Mengs (18th century). Opposite: Mexican painter Juan Urruchi portrays Potiphar's wife attempting to seduce Joseph in *Joseph and Potiphar's Wife* (1852).

thin, blighted ears of corn sprout and consume the fat ears.

Joseph explains that Egypt will face seven years of abundance followed by seven years of famine. Joseph recommends that Pharaoh appoint an administrator to oversee emergency preparations and to stockpile grain.

RISING TO POWER UNDER PHARAOH

Pharaoh is grateful and names Joseph overseer, giving him broad administrative powers to implement the proposed plan.

EGYPT THRIVES DURING FAMINE

Events transpire exactly as Joseph predicts, and when the famine comes, Egypt, with its stockpiles of grain, thrives while its neighbors suffer. Nearby in Canaan, Jacob hears rumors that the Egyptians have food. Hoping to purchase some for his family, Jacob dispatches his 10 eldest sons to the south, while keeping Benjamin at home.

The brothers reach Egypt, and after paying for their grain, they meet the responsible government official. That administrator is Joseph, but 13 years have passed and the

Jacob Blessing Joseph's Sons by Rembrandt (1656). Opposite: *Joseph Forgiving His Brothers for Selling Him into Slavery* by an unknown artist (20th century).

brothers don't recognize the now 30-year-old man. As they prostrate themselves before him, Joseph remembers his boyhood dream where his brothers bowed to him and decides to teach them a lesson.

In asking for Joseph's kindness, the brothers mention they have left their youngest member at home. Joseph accuses his siblings of being spies and demands proof that their story is true. He announces he will keep all 10 in prison until someone travels to Canaan and brings the young boy to Egypt. After locking the brothers up for three days, Joseph brings them out.

Joseph speaks in Egyptian and uses a translator to communicate with his brothers, who still don't realize who he is. But talking among themselves, the brothers agree they are being punished for how they treated Joseph many years ago. When he sees this sign of remorse, Joseph turns away, weeping. He releases nine of the brothers and tells them to return home to fetch Benjamin, their youngest brother. Joseph secretly returns the money the brothers paid for the grain and keeps the tenth brother, Simeon, in jail.

Arriving home, the brothers convince Jacob to allow Benjamin to return with them to see the administrator and set off for Egypt. But Joseph is not done with his tricks. This time, he hides a silver cup among Benjamin's possessions, and the boy is accused of theft. Joseph announces that in punishment, Benjamin must serve as his slave.

AN EMOTIONAL REUNION

Judah, the fourth-eldest, pleads with Joseph to release Benjamin and offers to serve as the slave instead. Joseph breaks down at this sign of self-sacrifice and reveals that he is their brother. He says he is not angry and that all the events were orchestrated by God to save them from starvation. He sends the brothers to retrieve their father, Jacob, and the rest of their families to live in Egypt for the duration of the famine.

Before Jacob dies, he blesses his 12 sons, calling them the tribe of Israel. He also blesses Joseph's sons Ephraim and Manasseh as if they were his own, doubling Joseph's inheritance at the expense of his brothers.

VERSES AND INSIGHTS

Why Joseph's brothers plot to kill him, and why Joseph forgives his siblings their betrayal

THE INTERPRETATION OF DREAMS
The ancients clearly distinguish between "everyday" dreams and those of a prophetic nature. Joseph's brothers may mock him and call him "Dreamer," but they recognize the significance of his visions and the need to put a stop to them before they come true. Jacob, having had a prophetic dream of his own, ponders the meaning of Joseph's dreams more deeply than his sons do.

JOSEPH AND FORGIVENESS
Just as Jacob and Esau put aside their differences and make up, Joseph, too, forgives his brothers for committing terrible wrongs against him and then lying about them to their father. Joseph spends years in prison because of his siblings and would be justified to use his power to exact revenge upon them. But he doesn't. He gives them what they denied him: mercy.

EXODUS 1–15; NUMBERS 1–4; DEUTERONOMY 5

Moses: The Leader of the Israelites

A prince of Egypt becomes a fugitive who frees the Israelites from Pharaoh's rule.

As Exodus opens, it is the worst possible time to be a Hebrew in Egypt. The people are slaves and have been for hundreds of years. They are forced to build cities and monuments by hand. Pharaoh, Egypt's leader, fears the population is growing too quickly and that it will rebel. To prevent an uprising, he issues a strict command to his people: "Every boy that is born to the Hebrews you shall throw into the Nile." (Exodus 1:22)

The Hebrew Jochebed, who has just given birth to Moses, defies Pharaoh's command. For three months, she keeps the infant's birth a secret. But as Moses grows, Jochebed knows it will be difficult to hide him forever. She places Moses in a basket and puts him in the Nile River. There, the infant is found by Pharaoh's daughter, who takes him to the palace.

Although Moses grows up as a privileged member of the royal family, he knows he is adopted and begins to suspect that he was born a Hebrew, not an Egyptian. At the palace, Moses hears rumors about the way the Hebrews are being mistreated, and when he turns 40, he decides to discover the truth for himself.

One day while out walking, Moses is horrified to see an Egyptian overlord beating a Hebrew slave. He jumps to the worker's defense, attacking and killing the Egyptian. Moses hides the man's body in the sand and assumes the worker will be grateful for the aid. During an incident the next day, Moses learns that word of the murder has spread, and he is terrified that Pharaoh will send soldiers to arrest him.

MOSES FLEES TO MIDIAN

Moses decides to flee and sets out for the land of Midian, several hundred miles away on the other side of the Sinai Peninsula. In a short time, Moses has gone from being a prince of Egypt to a fugitive far from home.

Moses arrives in Midian and stops at a well where seven sisters, the daughters of a priest, are watering their flock. The sisters invite Moses to meet their father, the priest Jethro, who offers the stranger a job as a shepherd. Soon, Moses joins the family by marrying one of the sisters, Zipporah.

ENCOUNTERING GOD IN A BURNING BUSH

Forty years pass. Moses, now 80, is with his sheep on the far side of Mount Horeb. Suddenly, he is startled by a bush that appears to be burning. It is an angel of the Lord.

Raphael's *Moses and the Burning Bush* (1513) at the Hermitage Museum, St. Petersburg, Russia.

As Moses draws closer to the bush, he hears God call to him. God identifies himself: "I am the God of your father, the God of Abraham, the God of Isaac, and the God of Jacob. I have observed the misery of my people who are in Egypt... I have come down ... to bring them up out of that land to ... a land flowing with milk and honey." (Exodus 3:6-8)

God tells Moses that he must return to Egypt to lead the Hebrews out of bondage. Moses protests that he is ill-suited for such a task, and in response, God bestows upon him a set of miraculous powers. Moses is now able to turn a staff into a snake and make his own hand leprous. These signs of God's might are to serve as a warning to Pharaoh to free the Hebrews or risk calamity for his own people. Moses remains reluctant, and God decides that Aaron, Moses's older brother, should also travel to Egypt to confront Pharaoh.

Once the brothers arrive at the palace and meet with Pharaoh, they both tell him that the God of Israel says, "Let my people go." Pharaoh replies, "Who is the Lord, that I should heed him and let Israel go?" (Exodus 5:1-2)

To underscore his power, Pharaoh orders the slave masters to stop giving the Hebrews straw for brickmaking, which makes it impossible for the workers to meet their quotas, but the Egyptians begin demanding even more bricks and beat the Hebrew overseers. In despair, the Israelite overseers protest to Moses and Aaron, and Moses goes to the Lord for answers. God tells him, "Now you shall see what I will do to Pharaoh." (Exodus 6:1)

Pharaoh is unaware of the wrath that is about to descend on him and all of Egypt.

MOSES AND AARON FACE PHARAOH

Pharaoh continues to doubt God's powers, forcing Moses and Aaron to use their staff to turn the water in the Nile to blood. The first plague kills the river fish, and their rotting smell spreads. Pharaoh refuses to believe that the Hebrew God is responsible for the horror and denies the people passage out of Egypt.

Seven days later, Pharaoh again rebuffs Moses and Aaron's demand to free the Hebrews. For the second plague, God instructs Moses to hold his staff out over the Nile. When he does, hordes of frogs fill the river and hop up onto the land. Pharaoh tells Moses that if he gets rid of the frogs, he will let the Hebrews go. But once the frogs vanish, Pharaoh reneges on his promise.

Eight more plagues are visited upon the Egyptians. After the ninth, Pharaoh banishes Moses from Egypt, telling him: "Get away from me! Take care that you do not see my face again, for on the day you see my face you shall die." (Exodus 10:28)

THE WORST PLAGUE OF ALL

After Pharaoh again refuses to let the Hebrews go, God unleashes a final, horrific plague: He calls for the slaying of all first-born Egyptian males.

The curse is so terrible that God gives Moses special instructions to prepare for it. Each Hebrew household is told to take a one-year-old male lamb or goat without defects, and on the 14th day of the month, to kill, roast, and eat it. In order to be "passed over" and spared, they are to use the animal's blood to mark the top and sides of their doorposts.

On the night of the 10th plague, the Hebrews follow all the instructions. They come to the table dressed and ready to travel. They eat in haste and wait for the Lord's command to leave Egypt.

At midnight, the 10th plague kills all the firstborn Egyptian males in Egypt. Not even the firstborn livestock are spared. Exodus 12 records that loud crying and wailing could be heard all over Egypt as firstborn males died.

THE HEBREWS LEAVE EGYPT

During the night, Pharaoh summons Moses and Aaron and orders all the Hebrews out of Egypt, where they have lived for 430 years.

As the people leave, Pharaoh changes his mind again and sends soldiers after them. When the Hebrews are camping at the edge of the Red Sea, they spot the Egyptian warriors approaching and panic because they have no escape route. Moses tells them not to fear.

A cloud the Hebrews have been following moves so that it separates them from the Egyptians. Throughout the night, the cloud shrouds the soldiers in darkness and provides light for the people.

Then Moses stretches out his hand over the Red Sea, and a pathway through the water opens up. The Israelites hurry through the divided waters to dry ground on the opposite bank. The Egyptians follow in their chariots, and God gives Moses a command: "Stretch out your hand over the sea, so that the water may come back upon the Egyptians." (Exodus 14:26)

Moses lifts up his arm, and the Red Sea closes over the Egyptian soldiers. The Israelites escape their captors and are finally free. But their journey has just begun.

GOD GIVES MOSES THE TEN COMMANDMENTS

After three months of travel, the Israelites arrive at Mount Sinai, where Moses meets with God, who announces he will make the Hebrews his chosen people if

At Moses's order, the waters of the Red Sea come together to cover Pharaoh's army in this work by an unknown artist (ca. 1900). Opposite: Moses lifts his staff to call down another plague in John Martin's *One of the Seven Plagues of Egypt* (1754).

they keep his covenant. Moses descends with the message and the people agree.

Three days later, a thick cloud covers Mount Sinai. Thunder rumbles and lightning flashes. A sudden blast from a trumpet startles everyone. In a blaze of fire and smoke, the Lord announces his Ten Commandments, but the sound of his voice so upsets the Hebrews that they beg Moses to receive God's orders alone. Moses sets off again to meet with the Lord.

Moses travels twice to the top of Mount Sinai, eventually staying for 40 days and nights, receiving more rules of conduct, the stone tablets inscribed with the Ten Commandments, instructions to build the Arc of the Covenant (to hold the tablets), and the tabernacle, a portable structure for the Arc and where God will speak to Moses when they are traveling in the desert.

THE ISRAELITES WORSHIP THE GOLDEN CALF

Uncertain why Moses is taking so long, the Hebrews go to Aaron and ask him to make golden idols for them to worship. Aaron agrees and casts gold into the shape of a calf. Aaron announces a ceremony for the next day. At the festival, the people worship the golden calf.

VERSES AND INSIGHTS

A Pharaoh and a feast

THE PASSOVER HOLIDAY

To help remember how God delivers them from the Egyptians, the Israelites begin to celebrate the Passover feast every year on the 14th day of the month of Nisan. During that week, the Hebrews refrain from all work except food preparation.

WHICH PHARAOH?

Scholars across many disciplines have long attempted to identify the Egyptian Pharaoh who Moses and Aaron encounter in Exodus. Among the candidates are the following:

Ahmose I
(1550–1525 B.C.)
Thutmose III
(1479–1425 B.C.)
Horemheb
(1319–1292 B.C.)
Ramesses I
(1292–1290 B.C.)
Ramesses II
(1279–1213 B.C.)

God observes the Hebrews and orders Moses down the mountain. Carrying the tablets, Moses begins the long descent. When he arrives at the camp and sees the people dancing around the gleaming statue, Moses smashes the tablets in anger. God tells Moses to climb back up Mount Sinai so he can write the Ten Commandments on two new stone tablets.

The Hebrews stay at Mount Sinai for several more months. During this time, the people build the Ark of the Covenant and the tabernacle.

MOSES SENDS SPIES INTO THE PROMISED LAND

God orders a census of his people and divides the Hebrews into 12 tribes based on ancestral families. The tribes are named after the 12 sons of Jacob, with two exceptions. The Levites are excluded from the count and are instead assigned the task of caring for the tabernacle and assisting with sacrifices. Similarly, God does not create a tribe named after Joseph, since Jacob adopted Joseph's two sons (Ephraim and Manasseh) as his own.

While the Hebrews camp in the Desert of Paran, the Lord tells Moses to send some men to explore Canaan. Moses selects one leader from each tribe for the expedition. Over the next 40 days, the men investigate Canaan and return to Moses with reports that the land is flowing with milk and honey.

Yet chaos ensues. One of the spies, Caleb, urges an immediate attack. The other men argue that the people there are too well armed. Some Hebrews are fearful and want to return to Egypt.

Angry that the Hebrews are hesitating, God says he should wipe them out and start over. Moses pleads on their behalf and says it would dishonor God's name if his people were destroyed. To punish the Hebrews for their lack of faith, God sentences them to wander the desert for the next 40 years.

FOR MANY, DEATH BY SNAKEBITE

At times, the people lose hope, fret, and rebel. The unrest offends God, and on one occasion, he sends venomous snakes into the camp where the Hebrews are staying. When many die of bite wounds, Moses asks God to remove the serpents. God tells Moses to make a model of a snake, put it on a pole, and walk through the camp. Whoever has been bitten and sees the pole will live.

Later, when the Hebrews reach Kadesh and water runs low, they complain to Moses again. Frustrated, Moses calls out, "Listen, you rebels, shall we bring water for you out of this rock?" (Numbers 20:10)

Though God has instructed Moses to only speak to the rock, he instead hits it twice with his staff and water gushes out. This act of disobedience angers God, who punishes Moses. Now Joshua, not Moses and Aaron, will lead the Hebrews into the Promised Land. Moses dies at the age of 120 on Mount Nebo in the land of Moab.

Moses destroys the sacred tablets after seeing the Israelites, in a painting by an unknown artist. Opposite: worshipping the golden calf. *The Adoration of the Golden Calf* from the *Loggia of Raphael*, Hermitage Museum, St. Petersburg, Russia.

WRITTEN IN STONE

The Ten Commandments are moral principles dictated by God

1. "I am the Lord your God, who brought you out of the land of Egypt, out of the house of slavery; you shall have no other gods before me." (Exodus 20:2-3)

2. "You shall not make for yourself an idol, whether in the form of anything that is in heaven above, or that is on the earth beneath, or that is in the water under the earth. You shall not bow down to them or worship them." (Exodus 20:4-5)

3. "You shall not make wrongful use of the name of the Lord your God, for the Lord will not acquit anyone who misuses his name." (Exodus 20:7)

4. "Remember the sabbath day, and keep it holy. Six days you shall labor and do all your work. But the seventh day is a sabbath to the Lord your God; you shall not do any work." (Exodus 20:8-10)

5. "Honor your father and your mother, so that your days may be long in the land that the Lord your God is giving you." (Exodus 20:12)

6. "You shall not murder." (Exodus 20:13)

7. "You shall not commit adultery." (Exodus 20:14)

8. "You shall not steal." (Exodus 20:15)

9. "You shall not bear false witness against your neighbor." (Exodus 20:16)

10. "You shall not covet your neighbor's house; you shall not covet your neighbor's wife." (Exodus 20:17)

JOSHUA 1, 4, 6, 9–18

Joshua: The New Moses

The Hebrews get a different leader.

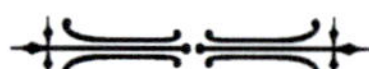

God is clear about Joshua's role as the new Hebrew leader. He instructs Joshua to "be strong and courageous" three different times in the opening verses and emphasizes the importance of obeying the laws given to the Hebrews through Moses.

Acting on God's admonition, Joshua sets in motion plans to invade Canaan. Joshua reminds the Hebrews that God promised to provide them with a land of their own and warns that they will have to enter as armed warriors to claim Canaan. The Hebrews accept Joshua as their leader and urge him on with God's words: "Only be strong and courageous." (Joshua 1:18)

Joshua sends two spies to see what the Hebrews will face in Jericho. The spies enter through the house of a prostitute, Rahab, who pleads with the men to spare the lives of her family. She acknowledges that the citizens of Jericho are terrified of the Hebrews and promises to keep their location a secret in exchange for saving her loved ones.

RAHAB HELPS THE HEBREW SPIES

Word of the spies reaches the king of Jericho, who sends soldiers directly to Rahab's house to capture the intruders. When the king's men pound on Rahab's door, she hides the Hebrews and lies to the soldiers, saying the pair must have snuck out through the city gates.

Grateful, the spies tell Rahab that when the Hebrews attack, she must gather her family into her home and hang a crimson cord from her window so they know which house to spare.

Hearing about the events in Jericho, Joshua is ready to proceed. He commands the camp's priests to carry the Ark of the Covenant and stop in the center of the Jordan River. When the priests wade into the river, the waters part, just as the Red Sea did for Moses, and

Anton Robert Leinweber portrays Joshua and the Israelite army in *Destruction of the Walls of Jericho* (1754).

the Hebrew army is able to cross safely.

Following orders from God, Joshua then selects one representative from each of the 12 tribes. He tells the men to place stones in the middle of the Jordan where the priests can rest the ark temporarily.

Once this work is complete, the priests may carry the ark to the far shore and let the waters rush back in. Joshua announces that in the future, people will see the stones and remember the miracle at the river.

Before the Hebrews enter the Promised Land, they must comply with a special covenant requiring the circumcision of all males born since the exodus from Egypt.

The ritual, outlined for Abraham in Genesis 17, is soon completed, and Joshua leads the people in the Passover feast, celebrating with food from their new land. This is the first day that the Hebrews don't have to rely on manna from heaven—a true sign that they have finally entered the land that God had promised to them.

TARGETING JERICHO

It is now time for the Hebrews to prepare for their first battle to capture Canaan. They have targeted the city of Jericho and will follow an unconventional plan of attack devised by God. Instead of ambushing the city with spears,

Joshua Passing the River Jordan with the Ark of the Covenant by Benjamin West (ca. 1800).

arrows, rocks, or swords, the priests of Israel will simply walk around the walls of the city for seven days. On the seventh day, seven priests will sound their trumpets, and the walls of Jericho will collapse.

The Hebrews enter the city, killing all in their path except Rahab and those in her household. They burn the city of Jericho to the ground.

THE SUN STANDS STILL

After the destruction of Jericho, the reputation of the Hebrews spreads rapidly. They are approached by the Gibeonites to make a peace treaty. Adoni-Zedek, the ruler of a rival kingdom, the Amorites of Jerusalem, forms an alliance with four powerful Amorite kings. This new alliance, called the five kings, makes plans to attack the city of Gibeon.

The Gibeonites hear that the five kings are preparing to besiege their city. They quickly send word to Joshua. Joshua rallies his troops, and after an all-night march, he and his army launch a surprise assault on the Amorites. To give the Israelites more daylight to fight by, God stops the sun in the sky over Gibeon for a full day.

The battle ends, Gibeon is saved, and the armies of the five kings are defeated.

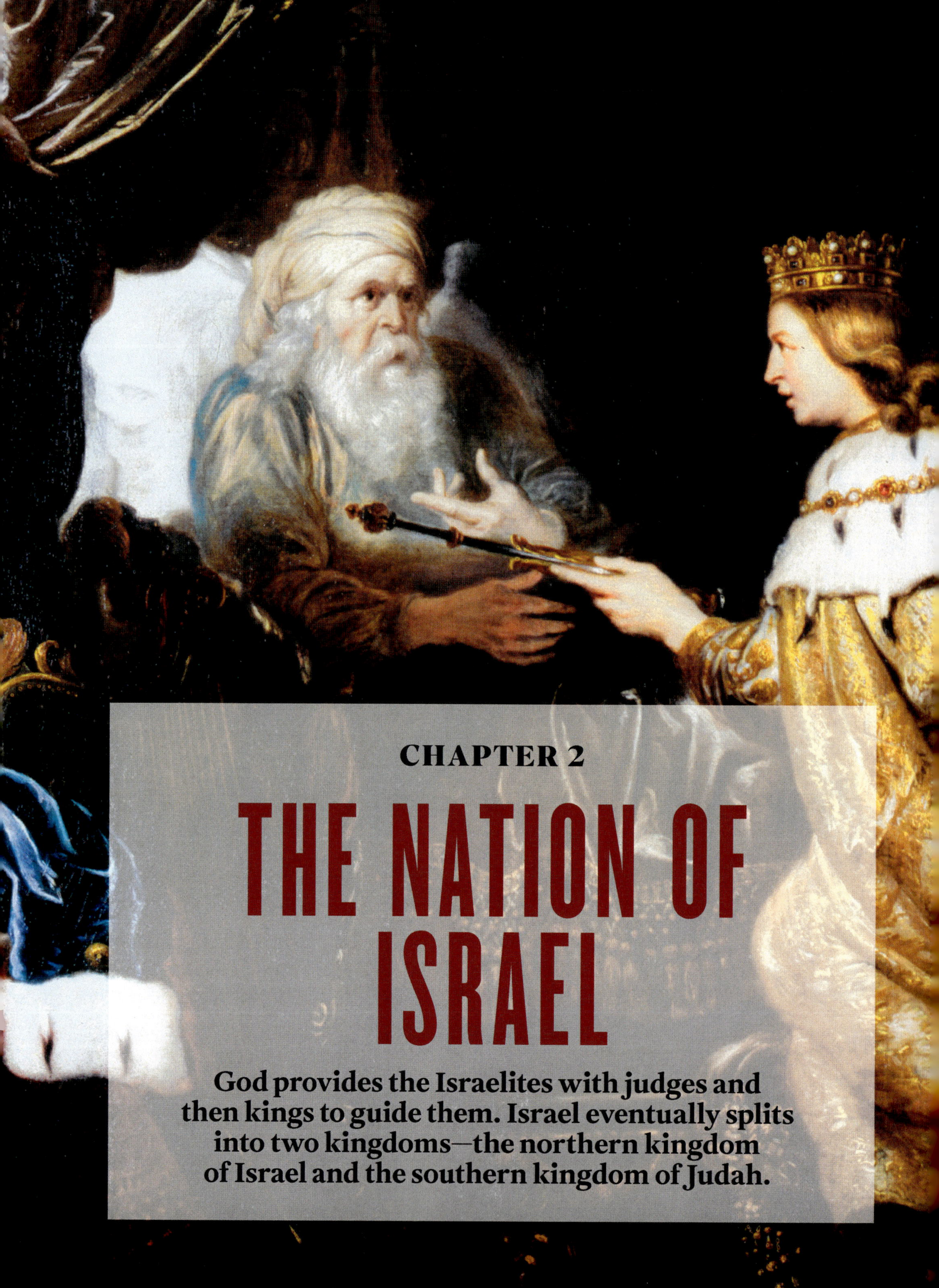

CHAPTER 2

THE NATION OF ISRAEL

God provides the Israelites with judges and then kings to guide them. Israel eventually splits into two kingdoms—the northern kingdom of Israel and the southern kingdom of Judah.

Power passes from father to son in *King David Presenting the Sceptre to Solomon* by Cornelis de Vos (ca. 17th century).

Jael drives a tent peg through the skull of the Canaanite commander in *Jael and Sisera* by Bartolomeo Guidobono (end of the 17th century).

JUDGES 4, 5

Deborah: The Only Female Judge

A brave and wise woman leads the Israelites to freedom from an oppressive king.

The book of Judges relates historical accounts of the Israelites taking over Canaan, with the Hebrews failing repeatedly to live up to their covenant with God. In this book, the people defeat the Canaanites over many years, but only after betraying God, surviving oppressors he sends, repenting, and returning to their faith.

Deborah is the only female judge mentioned in the Bible. She is called to deliver the Israelites from Jabin, the king of Canaan, who has oppressed the people for 20 years.

God tells Deborah to prevail upon Barak, the captain of the Israelite army, to challenge the commander of Jabin's forces in battle. In spite of the fact that Jabin and his troops have superior weaponry, including 900 iron chariots, the Israelite force of 10,000 follows Deborah's advice and is triumphant.

In her discussions with Barak, Deborah prophesies that the honor of killing the other army's general will be given to a woman. When Barak wins the battle, the losing general flees and seeks refuge in the tent of a young woman named Jael. With apparent goodwill, Jael "brought him curds in a lordly bowl." After the general drinks, he lies down and sleeps, and Jael drives a tent peg through his temple with such force that it enters the ground. Thus, Deborah's prophesy comes true. God allows a woman to kill the great general, the ultimate in humiliation for the Canaanites.

Deborah and Jael's victory is a turning point in the Israelites' battles with Jabin, and as Israel grows stronger, it eventually defeats him. Then there is peace for 40 years.

VERSES AND INSIGHTS

Again and again, the Israelites transgress, are punished by God, then are delivered by a judge

CYCLE OF WOE

This pattern, in which the Israelites abandon, then return to, their religion, is called the Cycle of Apostasy. Each time the people rebel against God and transgress, God punishes them with a trial, then sends a judge to deliver them. The people see their errors, cry out for help, and repent. As soon as the judge dies, the people do what is evil again, and the cycle repeats itself.

The book of Judges can be broken into four main sections:

1. Conquest
2. The Cycle of Apostasy
   - Sin
   - Punishment through foreign oppression
   - Repentance
   - Deliverance by a judge
3. The story of each judge
4. The fate of two of Jacob's sons, Dan and Benjamin

VERSE TO KNOW

"The Israelites again did what was evil in the sight of the Lord, after Ehud died." (Judges 4:1)

Gideon Surprising the Army of the Midianites by an unknown artist (1754). Left: Gideon chooses his 300 warriors after watching how they drink from the stream in *The Call of Gideon* by Arthur Dixon (ca. 1920)

JUDGES 6–8

Gideon: Reluctant to Serve

A new judge accepts his mission to lead the Israelites in defeating the Midianites.

Gideon is a reluctant judge, unsure of himself and of God's call to help the Israelites defeat their conquerors, the Midianites. Before he accepts his role, Gideon asks God to provide three signs. First, Gideon wants the angel of the Lord to cause a rock laid with an offering of bread and meat to burst into flames and to consume the sacrifice. Gideon then asks God to make his fleece rug wet with dew, while the ground is dry. Last, he requests the situation be reversed, so that the fleece is dry and the ground is wet. When God executes all these miracles, Gideon accepts his mission.

WHEN FEWER IS BETTER

God's strategy to defeat the Midianites is to have the conquering army turn on itself, a plan he orders Gideon to execute. Though more than 22,000 men volunteer to help the military leader in this battle, God wants to win using only a fraction of those soldiers to reflect his divine power. Gideon narrows his forces to 300 and provides each man with a shofar—a loud instrument made from a hollowed-out ram's horn—and a torch hidden in a clay pot. He instructs his troops to surround the enemy camp at night, and at a signal, to simultaneously break the pots, blow the

shofars, and blind the Midianites with torch light. The attack successfully disorients the enemy, who retreat.

The Israelites beg Gideon to become their king, but he refuses, asserting that only God is their ruler. He does, however, embrace his new power in other subtle ways. He fashions an ephod, or a priestly breastplate, out of the gold that is won in battle. Gideon also names one of his 70-plus sons Abimelech, which means "my father is king."

Peace prevails in Israel for 40 years, but as soon as Gideon dies of old age, the Israelites return to worshipping a false god.

THE ROLE OF THE SHOFAR

A shofar is a musical instrument, typically made of a hollowed-ot ram's horn, that is used for Jewish religious purposes. As with the modern bugle, the shofar does not have keys to control pitch. Instead, a player varies the lip position to coax sound from the horn. Traditionally, the shofar was used to mark the beginning of the new year and to announce holidays and the Jubilee year. It was also used to signal the start of a war or to send a message. Today, the shofar is blown on Jewish holy days.

JUDGES 13–16

Samson: Born with Supernatural Might

God uses Samson's strengths and weaknesses to bring judgment on the Philistines.

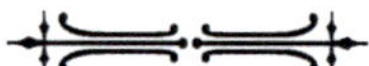

An angel comes to Manoah of the tribe of Dan and tells him that his wife is to refrain from alcohol because she is carrying a child who will be a Nazarite from birth and will free the Israelites from the Philistines. When the baby is born, the couple name him Samson, and the mother promises he will never drink alcohol, shave, or cut his hair as proof of his dedication to God. Thus, Samson is granted God's strength.

A WEAKNESS FOR WOMEN

Samson develops a weakness for Philistine women who betray him. The first is a woman from Timnah. On his way to propose marriage to her, Samson is attacked by a lion. With God's strength, Samson is able to kill the lion with his bare hands, and the woman agrees to be his wife.

Returning from their wedding, Samson notices that bees have made a nest in the carcass of the lion. He eats some of the honey and continues on to Timnah. After arriving, he composes a riddle for the Philistine groomsmen who are attending him. He makes a bet: If the groomsmen can't answer the riddle, they will have to pay him 30 linen garments. But if they do answer, Samson will have to pay them 30 garments. The men agree and he produces this riddle: "Out of the eater came something to eat. Out of the strong came something sweet." (Judges 14:14)

The groomsmen can't come up with an answer and blame the bride and her family for humiliating them. They tell her that if she doesn't get the answer for them, they will burn her and her family to death. The woman coaxes the answer out of Samson. When the groomsmen recite the answer for Samson, he flies into a rage and kills them all. Returning home to see his wife, Samson finds out her father has given her to another man. This sends him into another destructive rampage, burning the Philistines' crops.

SLAYS 1,000 WITH THE JAWBONE OF AN ASS

In retaliation, the Philistines burn Samson's wife and father-in-law to death. Samson escalates the conflict by killing thousands of Philistines. He is hiding in a cave when he is finally cornered by the Philistines. To save the 3,000 men who are trying to protect him, Samson gives himself up. But when he is in the middle of the Philistine army, he breaks his shackles, picks up a jawbone of an ass, slays 1,000 Philistine soldiers, and escapes.

Samson, in his final act as judge, in *Samson and Delilah and the Destruction of the Temple* by an unknown artist (ca. 19th century).

Samson soon meets Delilah, another Philistine woman, and falls in love again. Spies for the Philistines convince her to discover the secret to Samson's fierce powers. For many nights in a row, Samson tells Delilah a different story, but finally he admits the truth: His hair is the source of his strength. While her lover sleeps on her lap, Delilah allows the Philistines to cut his locks. For this, Samson is abandoned by God.

The Philistines seize Samson, poke out his eyes, and throw him in prison. He repents and regrows his hair, repairing his relationship with God. Preparing to publicly sacrifice Samson to their god, the Philistines bring him to the front of a temple. Crowds flock in to get a glimpse of the famous Samson and rejoice that he will die.

In his last act as a judge of Israel, Samson uses the strength God gives him to pull down the pillars of the temple, killing many Philistines who have gathered round, including all of their rulers.

DOWNWARD CYCLE

Time and again in the book of Judges, the Israelites break their covenant with the Lord, embrace the Canaanite gods, and are punished for their disloyalty.

In contrast, God is faithful throughout the book, and after sending in a conquering army to chastise his people when they stray, he goes on to deliver them from disaster. God is constant, not because Israel is deserving but because he is compassionate.

The judges, though, are no angels. Even as they rescue the Israelites, they often contribute to the downward cycle. Major judges such as Gideon, Jephthah, and Samson are guilty of significant sins, including hoarding gold and breaking vows to God, and only Deborah, the prophetess and warrior, proves to be the exception.

By the end of Judges, we see that Israel needs a king to lead in doing right in God's eyes rather than a leader who does "what was right in [his] own eyes." (Judges 17:6)

I SAMUEL

Samuel: A Promised Child

A late-life baby raised by a high priest becomes the last judge of Israel.

amuel, the last judge and the first prophet, serves an important transitional role between the judges and the kings.

The first book of Samuel begins with a description of a woman, Hannah, who is barren and miserable. She goes to the temple to pray to God for a child and is observed by Eli, a high priest. At first, Eli sees the woman's lips moving and thinks she is drunk. But upon hearing Hannah's words, he is moved by her sincere desire for a baby. When Hannah promises God that she will dedicate her child to him if she conceives, Eli blesses her. Hannah's prayers are soon answered and she names the baby Samuel. After he is weaned, she leaves the child in Eli's care.

GOD SPEAKS TO SAMUEL

Samuel is about 12 years old when he first hears God speaking to him. Initially he thinks the voice is Eli's, so he goes to the priest but is told to return to bed. After this happens three times, Eli realizes that God is speaking to Samuel. He instructs the boy to talk with God, who tells Samuel that Eli's sons, who have been sexually immoral and have disregarded the rules of sacrifice, are so wicked that Eli's dynasty will be condemned. Eli asks Samuel to honestly recount the conversation he has had with God. Though Eli has been aware of his sons' behavior, he has not removed them from their priestly duties. Hearing the bad news, Eli acknowledges that God should do what is right.

SAMUEL'S TURN

Once Eli dies, Samuel becomes a judge. He uses his position to fight the Philistines, to keep the Israelites focused on God, and to settle disputes among the people. But Samuel's sons, like Eli's, are corrupt, and the people are worried about submitting to their decisions. They demand that Israel be given a king.

Samuel opposes the appointment of a sovereign, explaining that a king will require males to fight in his army and will levy heavy taxes on his citizens. But when the Israelites insist, Samuel concedes.

He decides that the best way to choose the new ruler is to draw lots. Saul, the largest and strongest man in all of the tribes, is selected, and the people are temporarily satisfied. Later, Saul disobeys God's order to massacre the Amalekites, instead sparing the king and the best livestock. He loses favor with God, who asks Samuel to secretly anoint a future king.

Eli questions Samuel regarding his vision (artist unknown, ca. 1900). Opposite: The Philistines return the ark in *The Ark Sent Away by James Tissot* (ca. 1900).

RUTH

Ruth: A Loyal Daughter-in-Law

A grieving widow declares her allegiance to her mother-in-law.

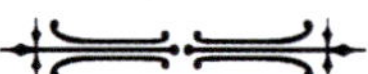

In this book, Ruth, a widowed Moabite, finds God through her first husband and his family. Hers is a story of love, loyalty, and hardship.

The narrative starts with a famine in Israel. Seeking food, Elimelech, his wife Naomi, and their sons, Mahlon and Chilion, emigrate from Bethlehem in Judah to the nearby country of Moab. In time, the sons marry two Moabite women: Mahlon takes Ruth as his wife, and Chilion pairs with Orpah. Soon after, however, all three men die.

Heartbroken and dejected, Naomi decides to return to Israel and tells her daughters-in-law to rejoin their own mothers and find new husbands. Orpah reluctantly goes to her family; Ruth, however, refuses, declaring to Naomi, "Your people shall be my people, and your God shall be my God." (Ruth 1:16)

Ruth and Naomi travel to Bethlehem, where it is the beginning of the barley harvest. Through her husband's family, Naomi has a wealthy kinsman named Boaz with a barley field. Since the two women have little to eat, Naomi asks Boaz if Ruth may trail his harvest workers and pick up kernels they leave behind, a practice known as gleaning. Boaz agrees and is kind to Ruth because he has heard about her loyalty to her mother-in-law. He tells Ruth he has asked the other workers to help her and that she should be rewarded for her deeds.

As a close relative of the family of Naomi's husband, Boaz is obliged by law to marry Ruth in order to carry on his family's inheritance. Eventually, Boaz and Ruth are married and produce a son named Obed, who is "the father of Jesse, the father of David." (Ruth 4:17)

Summer (Ruth and Boaz) from *Seasons* by Nicolas Poussin (ca. 1640).

Dutch artist Abraham Bloemaert's engraving shows Saul cut down in battle in *Death of Saul* (16th century).

I SAMUEL 8–11, 13

Saul: The First King

The Israelites demand a ruler for protection from other nations.

Scholars do not know how old the Israelite Saul is when he becomes king of Israel, nor how long he reigns. The Hebrew manuscripts are vague on this account. The text is clear, however, that the rule of Israel's first king was troubled from the beginning.

The narrative starts with the Israelites asking God for a human king who can protect them from other nations. God tasks the prophet Samuel with a search, but Samuel protests and tells the Hebrews that God too is opposed to the idea. In time, God overrides Samuel's objections and instructs him to select a strong warrior, and he chooses Saul. Saul's reign starts well when he defeats an Ammonite king who attacks the Israelite town of Jabesh. But preparing for another battle, Saul alienates Samuel by performing ritual sacrifices reserved for prophets. When Samuel arrives at the end of the ceremony, he tells Saul he will be replaced by someone who will do his duty and obey God. Over time, Saul listens less and less to God and Samuel. The relationship between Samuel and Saul is finally severed when Saul disobeys God's instructions to wipe out the Amalekites and their cattle. He instead takes the Amalekite king as a personal trophy and allows his men to keep cattle as their prize. Samuel withdraws his support of Saul and never sees him again. In a battle with the Philistines, Saul's three sons are killed, and he kills himself by falling on his sword.

Félix-Joseph Barrias shows the young David being chosen by God in *Anointing of David by Samuel* (1842).

I SAMUEL 16; 2 SAMUEL; PSALMS

David: The Great Leader of Israel

The son of a shepherd unites the people and creates a strong nation.

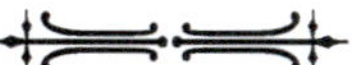

David is one of the most well known of all the biblical heroes. He is the youngest, smallest son of a shepherd; he famously kills a giant while still a boy; he is a gifted musician and writer; he is a handsome lady's man; he is a cunning general; and no matter how badly he behaves, he never seems to lose God's favor. During David's 40-year rule, he unites the people of Israel into a strong nation, conquers new lands, and paves the way for his son, Solomon, to build the temple.

David begins his ascent to power while Saul is still king. Without Saul's knowledge, God chooses a successor, one of the eight sons of Jesse of Bethlehem, the great grandson of Ruth. God sends Samuel to visit Jesse, who introduces him to his seven grown sons. Samuel, however, asks to see the youngest child, David, who is out with the sheep and who appears less impressive than his brothers. Instead, David is more faithful to God; Samuel then blesses the family and anoints David, who returns to his flock. It is said that the "Spirit of the Lord came mightily upon David" (1 Samuel 16:13) and at the same time deserted Saul. Suddenly tormented by a harmful or evil spirit, Saul seeks a musician whose playing might ease his affliction and bad temper. An attendant summons David and the king is pleased with what he hears. He keeps David close.

A BOY DEFEATS A GIANT IN AN EPIC BATTLE

The first time David publicly displays his courage is when, armed with only a stick and a few stones, he confronts an armored Philistine giant, Goliath of Gath.

At this time, it is common for an army to send out a

warrior to battle a member of the opposing force. Both factions agree that the winner will claim victory for his side.

It is David who volunteers to face Goliath after skilled warriors cower in fear for 40 days. Saul, the king, tries to suit the young boy up in armor and weapons, but none are small enough to fit him. Choosing to wear only his daily clothes, David makes a slingshot, invokes God's name, and kills the giant with his first shot, hitting him in the middle of his forehead. He then chops off Goliath's head, prompting the Philistines to flee in terror.

Impressed, Saul takes David on as commander of his troops. He initially calls David "my son," but in time grows jealous of the young warrior's successes.

DAVID BECOMES A SUCCESSFUL MILITARY LEADER

Saul watches with envy as David continues to triumph on the battlefield and vows to take his life—at one point he even enlists his son Jonathan in a plot. But Jonathan and David are friends, and Jonathan warns the military leader and tells him to escape. Finally, after multiple failed murder attempts, Saul declares a truce and makes a show of his goodwill by giving David his daughter Michal in marriage. But his hatred continues to seethe, and David ultimately is forced to flee Israel.

Finding refuge with the king of Moab, David begins a campaign to win support for his own army. He and his

David attacks the Ammonites in Gustave Doré's *Siege of Rabbah* (ca. 1870). Opposite: Italian painter Tiziano Vecelli (Titian) portrays David giving thanks after his victory in *David and Goliath* (ca. 1544).

band of men raid nomadic tribes and hand the spoils to the leaders of Judah. During this time, Saul and three of his sons are killed in a battle with the Philistines on Mount Gilboa. In spite of his history with the king, David mourns deeply. He moves to the city of Hebron in Judah, where the citizens are grateful that he saved them from the nomads and appoint David king of Judah.

David helps Judah become stronger than Israel. He is approached by the commander of Saul's army, Abner, who proposes an end to the rivalry between the kingdoms. David agrees, but then, without his permission, a rogue army commander kills Abner. Soon, another of Saul's sons, Ishbaal, is also murdered. David moves to unite Judah and Israel. The prophet Samuel, with the blessings of all the tribes of Israel, anoints David as their king.

David's first action is to capture Jerusalem, which became the City of David, to fortify it, and to build himself a palace. He moves the ark to Jerusalem and plans to erect a permanent temple where the Israelites may worship in safety. But God tells the new king that building it will be the job of David's son.

DAVID FALLS FOR BATHSHEBA

David shows great cunning and wisdom in leading his nation, but he is reckless in his personal life. One day while his men are away at war, David spies a beautiful woman,

Bathsheba, from his rooftop. He inquires about her and learns she is the wife of one of his generals, Uriah. David sends for Bathsheba, who conceives a child. At first David tries to fool Uriah into believing he is the father. He summons Uriah from war and suggests he return home. But Uriah refuses to lay with his wife while his men are still in battle. After Uriah foils David's plan, David arranges for Uriah to be killed during a dangerous mission so he can marry Bathsheba.

Nathan the prophet confronts David, who admits his sin. As punishment, Bathsheba's child dies and David is cursed with the promise of a rebellion from within his own house. Bathsheba and David soon conceive a second son, Solomon.

WRITING PSALMS TO GOD

David, along with being an able ruler, has a way with music and words. He is believed by some to have written close to half of the 150 sacred hymns that make up the book of Psalms, and many of the book's prayers are titled "A Psalm of David." One of the Dead Sea Scrolls attributes 3,600 songs of praise to this talented king.

The words of the hymns express David's everyday thoughts, struggles, and prayers. They describe scenes of hope and courage, as well as those in which David is forced to flee his enemies, needs strength and help, gives thanks for victories, asks for vindication, prays when his enemies defeat him, and prays for comfort.

Over the centuries, David's authorship has been called into question, with some biblical scholars suggesting that the ancients credited David as a way to link the psalms to divine inspiration. Today, it is widely believed the psalms were written over a time span of five centuries, from the early Canaanite period to the end of the Israelites' exile. The majority of the hymns originate in the kingdom of Judah, where they were sung during temple worship.

David plays the harp for his wife Michal in this painting by Virginio Grana (19th century). Opposite: David is enraptured by the beautiful Bathsheba in Jan Massys's *David and Bathsheba* (1562).

VERSES AND INSIGHTS

How tall was the giant really, and did King David's life foreshadow the coming of Jesus?

A GROWING LEGEND
With successive retellings of the David and Goliath tale, the giant has grown taller. The oldest manuscripts, including the Dead Sea Scrolls, the 1st-century historian Josephus, and the 4th-century Septuagint, all give Goliath's height as "four cubits and a span" (6 feet 9 inches). In later tellings, the giant's height is "six cubits and a span" (9 feet 9 inches).

VERSE TO KNOW
"Do not look on his appearance or on the height of his stature, because I have rejected him; for the Lord does not see as mortals see; they look on the outward appearance, but the Lord looks on the heart." (1 Samuel 16:7)

SHADOW IMAGE
Some believe that David foreshadows the life of Christ. Both men are born in Bethlehem; David is a shepherd while Christ is the Good Shepherd; David is betrayed by his trusted counselor Achitophel; Jesus is betrayed by his disciple Judas.

I KINGS 1–9

Solomon: The Third King

The son of David gains renown for his wisdom and fairness.

David promises Bathsheba that their son Solomon will succeed him on the throne, but as David's health begins to fail, his elder son Adonijah declares himself king. David orders his servants to bring Solomon to the Gihon spring so he can be anointed sovereign while David is still alive.

King Solomon assumes power in approximately 967 B.C., inheriting a kingdom that runs from the Euphrates River in the north to Egypt in the south. He becomes known for his wisdom, his wealth, and his writings, including the Song of Solomon, Proverbs, and Ecclesiastes.

FINDING THE TRUE MOTHER

One well-known story about Solomon's great judgment involves two prostitutes who live in the same house and bring him an infant. Both women had babies, but one has died in the middle of the night and each woman claims to be the mother of the surviving child. Solomon orders the baby be cut in two and that each woman receive half. One prostitute accepts the ruling; the other begs Solomon to let the child live, even if it is with her rival. Solomon determines that the true mother is the one who wants to spare the baby's life.

SOLOMON BEGINS CONSTRUCTION

Once Solomon's empire is tranquil, he begins to erect the temple based on the plans that God gave King David. He imposes compulsory labor service on both the Israelites and on the foreign nations under his control, and for seven years, the workers toil. When they are done, the edifice is unlike any other—made of stone, full of carvings, and overlaid with pure gold—and Solomon celebrates with a ritual ceremony of prayer and sacrifices.

Solomon also uses slave labor from the Hittites, Amorites, Perizzites, Hivites, and Jebusites on a multitude of other construction projects. He spends 13 years creating his own palace and also puts up a wall around Jerusalem, a citadel called the Millo, a palace for a favored wife, and facilities for foreign traders. He erects cities for chariots and horsemen and creates storage cities. He extends Jerusalem to the north and fortifies cities near the mountains.

MARITAL ALLIANCES AND TRADE RELATIONS

Solomon further solidifies his rule through marital alliances, trade relationships, and colonization. He has 700 wives and 300 concubines. He has a large share in the trade between northern and southern countries. He establishes Israelite colonies around his province to look after military, administrative, and commercial matters. He divides his empire into 12 districts, with Judah constitut-

In Francesco Podesti's *Judgment of Solomon* (19th century), the king determines an infant's true mother. Below: *Solomon's Palace and Temple in Jerusalem* by an unknown artist (ca. 1900).

ing its own political unit and enjoying certain privileges.

A myriad of forces contribute to Solomon's downfall in his old age. He allows his numerous foreign wives to worship other gods and make sacrifices; Solomon even builds an altar for them. He places heavy taxes on the people, who become bitter toward him. He forces his people to work as soldiers, chief officers, and commanders. The special privileges that had been granted to the tribes of Judah begin to alienate the northern tribes. Finally, the prophet Ahijah of Shiloh declares that Jeroboam, son of Nebat, is to become king over 10 of the 12 tribes—not one of Solomon's sons.

After 40 years of ruling Israel, Solomon dies and is buried in Jerusalem. His son Rehoboam takes over the remains of Solomon's empire. Under Rehoboam, the kingdom crumbles and finally is divided into two kingdoms: the northern kingdom of Israel and the southern kingdom of Judah.

JOB 1–38

Job: Tested by God

A righteous man suffers, argues with his friends, and is finally restored.

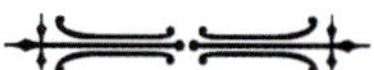

In the prose prologue to the story, Job is a prosperous and righteous man living in the land of Uz with his large family and flocks. One day, God points out to Satan that Job is a pious man. Satan responds that Job is good only because his life is going so well; if bad things were to begin to happen to him, Job would curse God. Disagreeing, God gives Satan permission to test Job's devotion as he wishes, short of taking his life.

Satan unleashes unthinkable punishments. He first kills Job's children and destroys his wealth. A bit later, he attacks Job physically, riddling his body with horrible boils. Even Job's wife turns on him, urging Job to "Curse God, and die," but Job refuses to do so. (Job 2:9). Instead, after these tragedies strike, Job tears his robe, shaves his head, and falls to his knees to praise the Lord as one who gives and takes away. Destitute and alone, Job is approached by three friends who attempt to comfort him.

The Book of Job **(ca. 11th century) from the Monastery of St. Catherine, Sinai, Egypt.**

From this point forward, the story is told in the form of poetic dialogues between Job and his friends and between Job and God. Job, as the protagonist, is praised for his steadfast defense of his own righteousness and God's justice and actions. Job's friends argue that he must have done something to incur the wrath of God. How, they argue, would God allow such a good man to suffer?

Though Job and his friends argue endlessly, there is no single victor. All make significant points and counterpoints using irony, sarcasm, and direct refutation.

As a storm gathers, God reveals himself to Job and asks: "Who is this that darkens counsel by words without knowledge?" (Job 38:2)

God then considers a list of mysteries so sublime and majestic he thinks Job and his friends cannot possibly understand them. The list includes the following:

- How land and water are balanced so perfectly on earth
- How the constellations such as Orion, the Pleiades, Arcturus, and the signs of the Zodiac are set in the night sky
- How animals have different gestation periods but all reproduce and grow
- How the Leviathan is so huge and ferocious

Job has no answer for God and, in the end, is satisfied that his Lord is just.

One conclusion to be drawn from these exchanges is that Job and his friends, because of their limited understanding and perspective, are unable to grasp the ineffable.

In the end, God restores to Job his former wealth. Job and his wife have more children.

The Division of the Kingdoms under Rehoboam **by William Hole (ca. 1899). Right: A map shows Israel's division into 10 tribes in two kingdoms.**

I KINGS 12; 2 CHRONICLES 10

Rehoboam: A Harsh Leader

A king loses control.

After Rehoboam ascends the throne, the people send an envoy under the leadership of Jeroboam, an exiled revolutionary, to ask for tax relief. The older counselors advise Rehoboam to lighten the load, to speak diplomatically, and to make himself a servant of the people. The younger counselors advise him to discipline and treat his subjects harshly, which is what the new king does.

The strict treatment drives all the northern tribes to secede from the kingdom, leaving Rehoboam with nothing but his own tribe of Judah. The northern alliance of tribes, called Israel, rallies around Jeroboam. His dynasty is brief, however.

After the death of Jeroboam, a series of short-lived kings follow one another in quick, bloody succession. Nadab, Baasha, Elah, and Ziri rise to power through violence and fall the same way. Ori, the captain of the army, succeeds Zimri, becomes king, and moves the capital to Samaria, where it remains for the rest of the kingdom.

VERSES AND INSIGHTS

Three accounts of the same events serve as a warning

1 & 2 KINGS, 2 CHRONICLES

1 Kings, 2 Kings, and 2 Chronicles cover the collapse of the united kingdom of Israel from different perspectives. The Kings accounts, thought to be written by the prophet Jeremiah, relate the history of both northern and southern territories and offer insight into the decline of a nation and its abandonment of religion. Chronicles, thought to have been written by the scribe Ezra, is about the kingdom of Judah only and serves to warn the people from repeating their mistakes.

I KINGS 16–18

Ahab and Elijah: A Battle Before God

A prophet challenges the followers of Baal to prove who is the true lord.

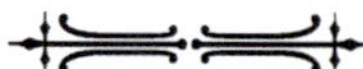

Succeeding Omri is Ahab, described as the most evil king in Israel's history. Ahab marries Jezebel, a princess who encourages him to import Baal worship, and takes a neighbor's land after conspiring to have him executed.

Offended by Ahab's behavior, God and the prophet Elijah seek to punish him. The episode starts when Elijah appears before the king and says, "As the Lord the God of Israel lives, before whom I stand, there shall be neither dew nor rain these years, except by my word." (1 Kings 17:1) Elijah then departs, leaving no word as to his whereabouts.

Elijah's prophecy to Ahab comes true; it stops raining. Three years into the drought, Elijah tells Ahab that he wants to arrange a battle between the God of Israel and Baal. Each side will build an altar and ask their god to send fire to burn the altar. The god who sends fire from heaven will be declared the true deity.

The followers of Baal build their altar and appeal all day to their god with no result. Elijah then soaks his altar with water and offers a simple prayer. His point is made when fire burns the water-soaked structure.

Elijah slaughters the prophets of Baal and tells the king to hurry to his palace before he gets caught in the storm.

The book of 1 Kings closes when Ahab is mortally wounded by an arrow in a battle, and the army deserts the field.

Prophets of Baal Sacrifice (ca. 1550–1560), a Belgian tapestry showing Elijah's sacrifice burning on the altar.

The Coronation of Joash and Death of Athaliah **by William Hole (ca. 1880).**

2 KINGS 11–12

Joash: A Child Ruler

An infant is protected and later becomes king of Judah.

The next king is Jehu, who purges all vestiges of Ahab in the northern territory of Israel. He even kills Ahab's grandson, Ahaziah, the heir to the Judean throne.

Athaliah, the mother of Ahaziah, is so enraged at the murder of her last surviving son that she goes on a bloody rampage. She kills all potential royal heirs she can find, hoping to forestall any conflict over the succession and then promptly places herself on the throne.

One heir who escapes Athaliah's slaughter is Joash, the infant son of Ahaziah. Joash and his nurse are rescued by the priest Jehoiada and hidden while Athaliah rules Judah for six years.

Eventually Jehoiada assembles a council to depose Athaliah and establish Joash as the rightful king when he is just seven years old. The queen rushes to the temple to accuse Jehoiada of treason, but he orders guards to seize her and to put her to death outside the temple grounds.

Under the regency of Jehoiada, Joash embarks on a series of religious reforms, restoring temple worship to its formerly prominent place. However, the reforms last only as long as Jehoiada lives because after his death, Joash lapses into apostasy.

After the death of Joash, a number of ineffectual kings preside over Israel's spiritual decline. The era is marked by idol worship, violence, and instability until the kingdom finally is forced into exile by Assyria around 723 B.C.

VERSES AND INSIGHTS

Understanding the differences between kings, priests, and prophets

FOLLOW WHICH LEADER?

In ancient Palestine, politics and religion are so deeply intertwined that it is nearly impossible when reading the Bible to separate them. This potent mix makes for an unexpected governmental structure. A king is the nation's top executive. His primary job is to lead his army in war, but he also adjudicates high-level disputes—usually of a civic rather than religious nature—that cannot be resolved by town and tribal elders. Priests are the descendants of Levi and have a complex mix of religious roles. Descendants of Aaron who perform ceremonial religious duties are considered priests. However, the rest of the descendants of Levi live throughout the land and serve in a support capacity. Priests interpret the law and settle disputes. Prophets answer a direct call from the Lord and serve as a check to excesses of the king or apostate priestly class.

Jonah and the Whale by Pieter Lastman (ca. 1610).

JONAH

Jonah: The One Who Refused

A prophet defies God but repents and is saved.

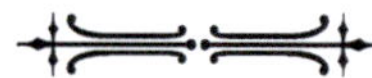

While there is a strong aspect of prediction in prophecy, Bible prophets do not exist simply to foretell the future. Their visions serve to underscore the main message of moral reform—the goal is to eradicate sin. Prophets are often royal advisers, but most are found working among the common people.

SENT TO NINEVEH

It's hard to talk about Jonah the prophet without mentioning the giant fish. Jonah's story, it seems, will be forever tied to the beast that swallows him.

The outline of the story is simple: God instructs Jonah to go to the city of Nineveh and tell the people that if they don't repent for their sinful ways, they will be judged.

Jonah refuses. Nineveh is the capital of the Assyrian Empire, foe to the Israelites, and Jonah does not want God to be merciful to the city's inhabitants. Instead, he heads in the opposite direction, to a port town, and boards a ship going to a remote destination.

Angry, God sends a violent storm that threatens to break up the ship. The sailors draw lots to determine the source of their bad luck and discover it is Jonah. They throw him overboard, where he is swallowed by a large fish sent by God. From the belly of the fish, Jonah repents, cries out to God, and is saved.

After three days and three nights, the fish deposits Jonah on the shore. He goes to Nineveh and preaches repentance. To his utter surprise, the people of Nineveh listen to him and are remorseful. God hears their contrition and spares them. Jonah, however, is bothered that the Ninevites are not judged. He complains to God, who tells Jonah that he should be concerned about the 120,000 people of Nineveh.

Many people miss the deeper meaning of the story of Jonah—about the ability to repent and be forgiven by God—when they get stuck on the plausibility of a big fish swallowing, then spitting out, a human. Jonah follows the Lord's call to preach judgment to a nation that will eventually destroy his own country. An even bigger miracle is that the Assyrians heed the message.

DANIEL 1–2

Shadrach, Meshach, and Abednego: In the Fiery Furnace

Three young Israelites stand up to King Nebuchadnezzar.

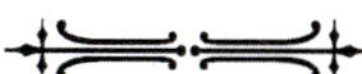

When Judah's ruler Zedekiah decides to withhold annual taxes from the empire, the Babylonian king, Nebuchadnezzar, orders the invasion of Judah and the decimation of Jerusalem. He sends the Jews into exile, the first time in at least 600 years that there is no nation of Judah.

While the Israelites are in exile in Babylon, King Nebuchadnezzar brings selected captives back to the kingdom to serve as liaisons between the subjugated peoples and the imperial court. Typically, he chooses the juvenile survivors of royal households for the task.

Daniel, Hananiah, Mishael, and Azariah are summoned to be schooled in the local language, in court manners, and in governmental administration. Daniel is renamed Belteshazzar; Hananiah becomes Shadrach; Mishael is Meshach; and Azariah becomes Abednego.

The four students win favor with the school administration, but that position is threatened when they refuse to eat meat from the imperial table because it isn't kosher. The men pass a performance trial while on their diet and are permitted to follow their dietary customs.

Throughout their service to the court, Belteshazzar, Shadrach, Meshach, and Abednego continue to fight for their traditions. In one instance, when they refuse to bow to an idol, Nebuchadnezzar threatens to burn Shadrach, Meshach, and Abednego to death. God intervenes and protects the three from the fire, prompting the king to allow the Jews to pray as they wish.

***Shadrach, Meshach, and Abednego in the Fiery Furnace* by an unknown artist (1863).**

DANIEL

Daniel: A Man with Dreams and Visions

God gives the prophet an amazing ability.

With the fall of the Babylonian Empire in 539 B.C. and the establishment of the Persian Empire 11 years later, a new king named Darius comes to power. Daniel serves and finds great favor with this king, causing the king's other advisers to become jealous. In a plot against Daniel, they persuade Darius to establish a new edict against praying to anyone but him.

In defiance of this edict, Daniel, an old man by this time, continues to pray daily to God. As punishment, he is imprisoned in a den of lions. When an angel intervenes, Daniel is spared and the advisers who promoted the royal law are fed to the lions instead. Daniel is permitted to continue his prayers.

A SERIES OF VISIONS

The book of Daniel contains a stunning series of visions, each one providing a detailed view of history. Here they are, presented in the same order as in the Hebrew Bible.

• **Nebuchadnezzar's Image:** Daniel sees a statue that he

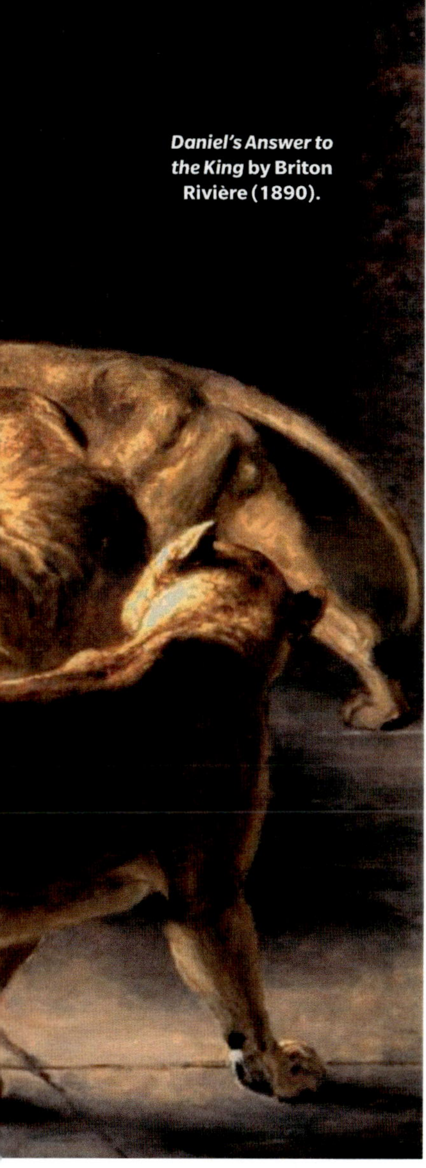
Daniel's Answer to the King by Briton Rivière (1890).

SECULAR RULERS DURING THE EXILE AND RESTORATION

DATE (B.C.)	SECULAR RULER(S)	EVENTS
606–562	**Nebuchadnezzar**	Events in Daniel 1–4, including the fall of Jerusalem, deportation of Jews to Babylon, and destruction of the temple
562–560	**Evil-merodach**	Release of Jehoiachin from prison
556–539	**Nabonidus** **Belshazzar**	Events in Daniel 5, including the conquest of Babylon by the Medo-Persians
539–522	**Cyrus** **Cambyses**	Events in Ezra 1–3, including the return of first exiles to Jerusalem and the beginning of the rebuilding of the temple
521–486	**Darius the Great**	Second decree to rebuild the temple Events in Ezra 6–10, including the end of construction and dedication of the temple
485–465	**Ahasuerus**	Events in the book of Esther, including the banishment of Vashti, the rise of Esther as queen, and the foiling of Haman's plan to destroy the Jews
465–424	**Artaxerxes I**	Events in the book of Nehemiah, including the return of exiles under governorship of Nehemiah and the rebuilding of the wall around Jerusalem

Legend: Babylonian Empire · Persian Empire

says represents a succession of kingdoms. Its head is of gold, symbolizing Nebuchadnezzar. The statue's other body parts are fashioned from silver, bronze, iron, and clay, indicating rulers who will succeed Nebuchadnezzar.

• **Handwriting on the Wall:** Daniel describes a hand that writes on the palace wall in an unknown language during a feast of Belshazzar, the last king of Babylon. Daniel interprets the writing as announcing the fall of the Babylonian kingdom.

• **Creatures from the Sea:** In a dream, Daniel sees four animals emerging from a body of water: a lion, a bear, a leopard, and an unidentified beast with iron teeth and 10 horns. Daniel interprets this to mean four kingdoms, which scholars believe represent Babylon, Persia, Greece, and Rome. The dream is thought by scholars to foreshadow the rise of God as ruler of the earth.

• **Ram and the Goat:** Daniel dreams of a ram that is attacked and killed by a goat with a conspicuous horn. The horn then splits into four unique horns that grow toward the four corners of the earth. This passage has been interpreted by scholars as representing the defeat of the Persian Empire under its first king by the Greeks and the division of the kingdom into four.

• **Seventy Weeks:** One of the most controversial visions in the book of Daniel, this dream involves the rebuilding of the temple, reestablishment of sacrificial worship, the coming and destruction of "an anointed one," and the subsequent destruction of the city and the temple. The timing and meaning of these events are widely disputed among various Jewish and Christian traditions. Some see the "anointed one" as Cyrus; others think it refers to Jesus.

• **Kings of the South and the North:** Chapters 10–12 of Daniel contain a complicated story of conflicts between the kings of the north and the kings of the south. The passages often are interpreted by scholars as a prophecy of the wars between the Selucid kings in Asia Minor and the Ptolemaic kings in Egypt. Some think the chapters predict the rise of Rome under Mark Antony and Cleopatra.

ESTHER

Esther: A Jewish Queen

The young prophet risks her life for her people.

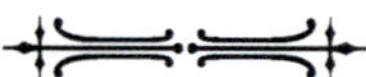

During this period of exile, Ahasuerus becomes the king of Persia in Babylon. Three years into his rule, Ahasuerus hosts a banquet and commands his queen, Vashti, to appear in front of his male guests. Vashti refuses, prompting Ahasuerus to banish her. He orders his officials to bring the most beautiful young women of the kingdom into his harem so that he may choose a replacement.

Mordecai, a palace functionary and Jew, suggests to his cousin Hadassah that she present herself to the keeper of the harem as "Esther" (meaning "Star") but that she keep her religion secret. Not only is Esther taken into the harem, but she becomes the king's favorite and is appointed queen.

Soon, Mordecai foils a plot to assassinate the king and rises in the palace ranks until he crosses Haman, Ahasuerus's highest official. By refusing to bow to Haman, Mordecai infuriates the king's aide and becomes the subject of a plot himself. Learning that Mordecai is a Jew, Haman convinces Ahasuerus to order the extermination of all Jews in the kingdom. The slaughter date is set a year ahead so that Haman will have time to execute the plan.

SPEAKING TO THE KING

Within a short time, Mordecai persuades Esther to intercede and save her people. She does so at the risk of her own life by entering the king's presence unbidden and inviting Ahasuerus and Haman to a series of dinners. On the second day of feasting, Esther reveals that Haman has tricked the king into signing a decree that will result in her death and in the death of all Jews. Enraged, the king orders Haman to be hanged on the gallows that Haman had ordered to be custom-built for Mordecai.

Yet even with Haman gone, Ahasuerus cannot rescind his decree. Instead, he issues a counter-proclamation calling for the Jews to take up arms and defend themselves from any who would execute the king's original order, thus rescuing the Jewish people from annihilation. The Jews rejoice at their change in fortune.

Queen Esther accuses Haman in this illustration by Arthur Dixon (ca. 1915). Opposite: Esther risks her life by entering the throne room of the king unbidden in *Esther and Ahasuerus*, by an unknown artist (ca. 1775).

Ezra Reading the Torah, illustration from L'Histoire Sainte, Paris (late 19th century). Opposite: Julius Schnorr von Carolsfeld depicts the laying of the foundation stone for the temple in Jerusalem (late 19th century).

EZRA; NEHAMIAH

Ezra and Nehamiah: A Scribe and a Governor

The two men work to bring back religious observance and to rebuild the temple.

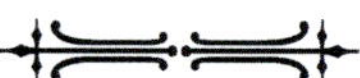

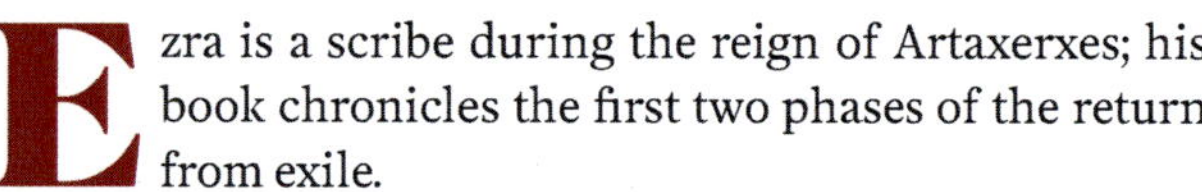

Ezra is a scribe during the reign of Artaxerxes; his book chronicles the first two phases of the return from exile.

Chapters 1–6 of Ezra describe how King Cyrus commissions the rebuilding of the temple in Jerusalem and sends Zerubbabel, a governor in the Persian province of Judah, and Jeshua, the high priest, to lead a first contingent of exiles back to the land. These leaders start the work of rebuilding the altar and reinstitute the observance of Sukkot (the Feast of Tabernacles).

The Samaritans and other local inhabitants, who are alarmed by the return of the Israelites, challenge the work of Zerubbabel and Jeshua and write to the king to bring the temple construction to a halt. After some negotiations, Cyrus's emissaries are allowed to continue their work.

In chapters 7–10, Artaxerxes commissions Ezra to appoint officials to administer justice to the returning exiles. The scribe and a large number of Israelites leave for Jerusalem, taking with them vast wealth to use in the service of the Lord. Upon returning, Ezra discovers that some recent arrivals have married local non-Jewish women. Disturbed by the interfaith marriages, Ezra confronts the offenders and orders them to send away their foreign wives and children.

WALLS OF THE CITY IN HOPELESS DISREPAIR

Nehemiah, an official to the Persian court, is appointed governor of Judea by Artaxerxes and is sent to Jerusalem to administer justice to the people in the emperor's name.

Upon arrival, Nehemiah inspects the walls of the city and finds them in hopeless disrepair. He commissions a workforce to begin fortifying Jerusalem. Because of interference by some local people, the work proceeds slowly. Eventually, Nehemiah arms the workers and they are able to complete the work of building the city walls.

As governor, Nehemiah institutes both civil and religious reforms, including tax relief, elimination of the governor's stipend, an end to cronyism, and the cancellation of debts and mortgages. He also calls for a public reading of the Torah by Ezra and the reestablishment of the traditional feasts under the direction of a rededicated priesthood.

After 12 years of improvements, Nehemiah returns to the Persian capital in Susa.

Time passes, and Nehemiah hears that the priest Eliashib has installed his family in richly appointed apartments of the temple instead of using the facilities to help the Levites. Nehemiah gets permission from Artaxerxes to return, and when he arrives, he stops the corrupt practices.

CHAPTER 3

JESUS AND HIS DISCIPLES

One of history's greatest figures grows up in a humble home, then leaves it at age 30 to begin his ministry. His disciples later spread the Gospel message.

Stained glass window inside the Madison Avenue Baptist Church in New York City.

MATTHEW; MARK; LUKE; JOHN

Matthew, Mark, Luke, and John: The Gospel Writers

The Gospels tell us most of what we know about the Son of God.

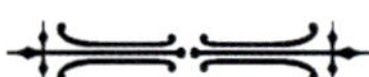

Who exactly was Jesus? Each of the four Gospel writers has his own unique approach to answering this question.

•**Matthew** (also called Levi, former tax collector and apostle) focuses on Jesus as king and Messiah. Writing for his fellow Jews who are familiar with the Old Testament, Matthew fills his Gospel with Old Testament messianic prophecies that are fulfilled in Jesus's life. He begins by tracing Jesus's legal bloodline through his adopted father, Joseph, back to Abraham. This genealogy is unusual because, in addition to Mary, it includes Ruth, a Gentile, plus three women who committed sexual sin: Tamar, Rahab, and Bathsheba.

•**Mark** (collaborated with Peter and Paul and founded the church of Africa) writes the shortest and most action-packed Gospel, probably intended for a Roman audience. He emphasizes Jesus as a suffering servant. Some believe Mark is the naked streaker who runs away when Jesus is arrested. (14:51-52)

•**Luke** (Gentile physician and companion of Paul) is the only Gospel writer who didn't know Jesus personally. Instead, Luke carefully compiles his account through investigation and interviews with individuals who spent time with Christ, such as his mother, Mary. Luke focuses on Jesus's parables, teachings, and miracles. He writes what most scholars believe is Jesus's biological genealogy, starting with Mary and reaching back to forebears such as David and Adam.

•**John** (former fisherman and part of Jesus's inner circle of disciples) completes his Gospel about 30 years later than the other writers, so his approach is quite different. John mentions seven miracles but focuses on the ones that show Jesus is God's Son, such as the episode in which Jesus raises Lazarus from the dead. (11:1-44) John's Gospel includes a famous Bible verse: "For God so loved the world that he gave his only Son, so that everyone who believes in him may not perish but may have eternal life." (3:16)

The Holy Family, with Saint Elizabeth (left), Saint John the Baptist (kneeling in front), and two angels, by Anton Raphael Mengs (1749). Opposite: *St. Luke at His Desk* by Andrea Mantegna (1453–1454).

The Nativity at Night by Guido Reni (1640).

MATTHEW 1; LUKE 1, 2

Mary: The Mother of Jesus

A young girl from Judea learns she will bear the Son of God.

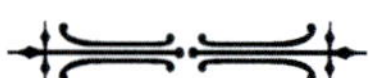

The miraculous events surrounding Jesus's birth start with a couple in Judea: a young virgin named Mary and her fiancé, Joseph.

GABRIEL'S MESSAGE

The story begins with an unexpected visitor. The angel Gabriel appears to Mary, who is startled when the angel tells her she is favored by God and will become pregnant and give birth to a son to be called "Son of the Most High." (Luke 1:31) Mary asks how this will be possible, since she is a virgin. Gabriel explains that the Holy Spirit will come upon her and overshadow her, so that the child will be called the Son of God. Mary accepts Gabriel's words and responds, "Here am I, the servant of the Lord." (Luke 1:38)

Although distressed to learn his young fiancée is pregnant and not by him, Joseph is pacified when an angel tells him in a dream, "Do not be afraid to take Mary as your wife, for the child conceived in her is from the Holy Spirit."

Before the baby's birth, Joseph and Mary head to the town of Bethlehem in order to register for a census. During their stay in Bethlehem, Mary delivers baby Jesus and marvels at the events that surround his arrival.

VERSES AND INSIGHTS

Different views about Mary, and why the Gregorian calendar, based on Jesus's birthday, is off a few years

THE MARY DEBATES

Christian communities around the world venerate Mary, but there is sharp theological debate about her role. Some Protestants see Mary simply as the mother of Jesus and her role as limited to giving physical birth. Other traditions, such as Catholics, Orthodox, and Copts, believe that as the mother of Jesus, Mary was also the Mother of God. These communities have theologies and practices specifically around Mary, such as Catholics saying the Rosary.

MATH ISSUE

In the 6th century, historian Dionysius proposed basing the calendar on Jesus's birth and labeled years after that day Anno Domini, or A.D. However, Dionysius miscalculated the year Herod died, which we now know was 4 B.C. Jesus would have been born before that, so the calendar is off by four to six years.

MATTHEW 3; MARK 1; LUKE 1, 3; JOHN 1

John the Baptist: Preparing the Way for Jesus

John's public ministry alerts the people to the coming Messiah.

Before the start of his public ministry, John can be found with his elderly parents, Zechariah and Elizabeth, in Ein Karem, a village near Jerusalem. He has known from a young age that his life's task will be to ready the world for the coming Messiah, a responsibility that was foretold by Zechariah. "And you, child, will be called the prophet of the Most High; for you will go before the Lord to prepare his ways." (Luke 1:76)

John spends time in the wilderness of Judea and then moves close to the Jordan River to fulfill his mission. With his long, uncut hair, powerful voice, strange attire, and compelling call to repent, John attracts streams of listeners as he delivers his message. Many people respond and want to be cleansed of their sins, and John proceeds to baptize them in the Jordan. At the same time, he begins to alert the crowds that the Messiah will be appearing soon.

John baptizes Jesus in Francesco Trevisani's *The Baptism of Christ* (1723).

JESUS REASSURES JOHN

At age 30, knowing it's time to begin his vocation, Jesus leaves Nazareth and heads to the Jordan River, where John is baptizing people. When John sees Jesus, he protests: "I need to be baptized by you, and do you come to me?" (Matthew 3:14) Jesus reassures him it is important to meet all of God's requirements. John agrees to perform the rite, and Jesus enters the Jordan River.

After John baptizes Jesus, the heavens open as the Holy Spirit descends in the form of a dove. When the bird lights on Jesus, a voice from heaven speaks: "This is my Son, the Beloved, with whom I am well pleased." (Matthew 3:17)

In John 1:32-34, John the Baptist testifies to the people that God has informed him that he will know the Messiah when he sees the Holy Spirit come down on him. From this moment on, John openly declares that Jesus is the Messiah.

This panel from a huge tapestry by Raphael (ca. 1515) hangs in the Sistine Chapel and depicts Jesus's charge to Peter, "Feed my sheep."

MATTHEW; MARK; LUKE; JOHN

Jesus: The Son of God

A miraculous birth is followed by a world-changing ministry.

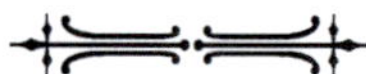

Only two Gospels—Matthew and Luke—discuss Jesus's birth, and the amazing events they record are fitting for a newborn king and Savior.

BRIGHT ANGELS ON A DARK NIGHT

Luke's account of angels appearing to shepherds on the night of Jesus's birth gives early clues of who Jesus will become. The first angel says, "Do not be afraid; for see—I am bringing you good news of great joy for all the people: to you is born this day in the city of David a Savior, who is the Messiah, the Lord." (Luke 2:10-11)

Then a host of angels fills the sky, singing glory to God. When the angels leave, the shepherds hurry into the small town of Bethlehem, just outside of Jerusalem, and find the baby as described. After viewing him with wonder, they spread the news of all they have seen and heard.

VISITORS FOLLOW A STAR FROM AFAR

Some foreign astrologers, known as Magi or wise men, spot an unusual star in the sky. Instinctively, they know a king of the Jews has been born and they follow the star to Jerusalem, the capital, as the most likely birthplace. The Magi visit the local ruler, King Herod, to ask about this omen. Herod is frightened by the prospect of a new king coming to replace him, and he asks the Magi to return with news after they find the infant. Herod claims he wants to pay his respects to the new king of the Jews, but his real plan is to murder the baby.

Warned in a dream of the deception, the Magi follow the star to the exact location of Jesus's family, just south of Jerusalem, in Bethlehem. They honor the new king with gifts of great value: gold, special incense used for worship, and myrrh, an oil used for burial. After delivering these gifts, the Magi continue their journey but do not return to Herod. Enraged that the wise men do not come back to him, Herod orders all the baby boys under the age of two in Bethlehem killed. Jesus, however, escapes because an angel tells Joseph to take his family and flee to Egypt.

A NORMAL FAMILY LIFE

Jesus grows up living a quiet life with his family in the town of Nazareth. According to Matthew 13:55-56, he has four younger half-brothers and several half-sisters. Since Joseph is a carpenter, Jesus learns the trade and works on projects such as making yokes and building furniture.

JESUS'S MINISTRY BEGINS

At the age of 30, Jesus leaves Nazareth and heads to the Jordan River, where he is baptized by John the Baptist. His baptism marks the beginning of his three-year ministry.

THE SERMON ON THE MOUNT

The first time Jesus addresses the masses, he delivers some of his most memorable lessons in a discourse known as the Sermon on the Mount. First-century Jews attending synagogue on the Sabbath are unprepared for Jesus's new approach. He does not mimic the scribes' painstaking references to scripture but appears to rely on his own authority. Many common people love his fresh approach to Jewish questions, but there are scholars who are disturbed by the implications regarding his identity.

AMAZING MIRACLES

Jesus also performs miracles—including faith healings, exorcisms, resurrections and control over nature—that amaze the people following him. The Gospels record Jesus performing more than 30 distinct miracles. The English word miracle is derived from the Latin "miraculum" and means "something that is wondered or marveled at." The miracles recorded in the Gospels do more than cause awe or amazement; they demonstrate divine or supernatural activity at work.

Jesus uses a variety of methods to heal, depending on the person's needs and level of faith. He relieves people who are in severe pain, cures seizures, and reverses paralysis. He gives sight to the blind, restores a shriveled hand, heals leprosy, and makes the lame walk. He casts out demons and brings people back from the dead.

While there are other miracle workers at the time of Jesus, none of their wonders compares to his greatest demonstrations of power over nature: turning water into wine, feeding 5,000 people with five loaves of bread and two fish, calming a storm, and walking on water.

Jesus calls Peter and Andrew to "fish for men" in Duccio di Buoninsegna's *Vocacion de los Apostoles Pedroy Andres* (ca. 1308).

MATTHEW 4, 9, 27; MARK 3, 14; LUKE 5, 6; JOHN 1, 18

Andrew, Philip, Nathanael, and Judas: Four Disciples

Jesus calls 12 men who will be with him for three years.

As Jesus begins to travel around the countryside preaching, a crowd trails behind, eager to hear his message. Like him, they are Jews. Some follow Jesus spontaneously, while others receive personal invitations. Over time, Jesus gets to know his followers and begins identifying those he wants as his disciples to help spread God's word.

ANDREW HEARS AND FOLLOWS

John the Baptist identifies Jesus as the Messiah and, with another man, begins to heed Jesus's words. Andrew, one of John's disciples, convinces his brother Simon (eventually renamed Peter) to come meet Jesus by telling him, "We have found the Messiah." (John 1:35-42)

PHILIP IS INVITED

In contrast, Jesus reaches out to Philip directly, saying, "Follow me," and Philip does. Philip, in turn, approaches his friend Nathanael, who is skeptical that anyone from Nazareth could have wisdom worth hear-

The Kiss of Judas (1303–1305) by Giotto, from the cycle of frescoes in the Scrovegni Chapel, Padua, Italy.

ing. He quickly changes his mind once he meets Jesus. (John 1:43-51)

THE 12 DISCIPLES ARE CALLED

Before Jesus formally identifies his disciples, he spends the night praying for guidance. In the morning, Jesus calls together his large group of followers and from them selects 12 men: Peter; Andrew; James; John; Philip; Bartholomew; Matthew; Thomas; James, son of Alphaeus; Simon the Zealot; Judas, son of James; and Judas Iscariot. This group will live with and learn from Jesus over the next three years.

JUDAS BETRAYS JESUS

The most infamous of Jesus's disciples is Judas, who agrees to identify Jesus in exchange for 30 pieces of silver. Working for the high priest Caiaphas, Judas arranges a signal: The one he kisses is the one to be arrested. While Jesus is praying in the garden of Gethsemane, Judas leads a crowd of armed guards into the garden. Judas goes up to Jesus and kisses him. Jesus is arrested and taken before Pilate.

After Jesus is condemned to death, Judas repents of his betrayal and, in his grief, kills himself.

VERSES AND INSIGHTS

The model for Jesus's relationship with his disciples

VERSE TO KNOW

"Jesus said to them, 'Follow me and I will make you fish for people.' And immediately they left their nets and followed him." (Mark 1:17-18)

A STUDENT-TEACHER RELATIONSHIP

Jesus's relationship with his disciples follows Jewish traditions of the era. A rabbi in 1st-century Judea was a scholar who had spent his life studying Hebrew scriptures to discover how to live to please God. Some rabbis led congregations; others were teachers. A young man who became a rabbi's disciple would be expected to submit to the rabbi's authority. The rabbi and his disciples would live together and discuss every aspect of their daily lives.

MATTHEW; MARK; LUKE; JOHN

Jesus: Suffering and Leading

For claiming to be the Son of God, Jesus is accused of blasphemy and is crucified. He returns to earth with instructions for his disciples to spread the word

JESUS'S TEACHINGS REVEAL HIS IDENTITY

Throughout his ministry, Jesus's claims of divinity, having a special relationship to God, or having the same powers as God, anger some of the Jewish leaders, who treat him as a sinner and blasphemer. Here are a few examples.

• **The power to forgive sins:** While Jesus is teaching in Capernaum, four friends bring a lame man to him to be healed. Instead of curing the man, Jesus says, "Son, your sins are forgiven." (Mark 2:5) Jewish leaders, hearing the comments, consider Jesus a blasphemer as he is claiming the same powers as God. Knowing their thoughts, Jesus asks, "Which is easier, to say to the paralytic, 'Your sins are forgiven' or to say, 'Stand up and take your mat and walk'?" (Mark 2:9) To show the scholars that he can do both, Jesus proceeds to heal the man.

• **Calling himself the "Son of God":** While in Jerusalem on the Sabbath, Jesus heals another man who is lame. When the Pharisees accuse Jesus of working, thus breaking Sabbath law, he answers, ". . . for whatever the Father does, the Son does likewise." (John 5:19) By speaking about God as his Father, Jesus angers the Pharisees, who think he is making himself equal to God.

• **He claims eternal existence:** In a discussion with the Jews about Abraham, Jesus states that Abraham was glad to see Jesus's day. When they exclaim, "How could you see Abraham?" Jesus says, "Before Abraham was, I am." (John 8:57-58) The Jews understand that "I am" is how God identified himself to Moses. (Exodus 3:14) They think Jesus is saying he has always existed and will always exist, just like God.

JEWISH LEADERS PLOT TO KILL JESUS

As Jesus's ministry progresses, the Pharisees become more worried by his miracles, apparent claims, and increasing popularity. When some report to the Pharisees that Jesus was in Bethany and raised a man named Lazarus from the dead, the Pharisees consult with a rival religious group, the Sanhedrin. The two groups convene a council to discuss the events at Bethany. They worry that if they let Jesus go on like this, the Romans will come and destroy the temple and the entire Jewish nation in order to stamp out Jesus's influence.

Rather than risk the fate of all Jews, Caiaphas, the Sanhedrin high priest, says it would be better that Jesus "should die for the people." (John 11:50) The Jewish authorities agree and plan to seize him when he arrives in Jerusalem for Passover.

ENTERING JERUSALEM

On the Sunday morning before Passover, Jesus enters Jerusalem riding on a colt that his disciples have brought to him. The Passover crowds see him coming and happily

Jesus Healing a Paralytic at Capernaum **by an unknown artist. Opposite: Marco d'Oggiono's *The Last Supper* is a copy from the 16th century of Leonardo da Vinci's masterpiece.**

join the procession, throwing their garments in front of him and waving palm branches.

THE LAST SUPPER

Jesus foresees the suffering he is about to endure and uses his final meal to prepare his disciples for what is about to happen. Relying on two elements of the Passover meal—the unleavened bread, or matzah, and wine—Jesus first picks up the unleavened bread, gives thanks, breaks it into pieces, and hands a bit to each disciple. Then he says, "This is my body, which is given for you. Do this in remembrance of me." He then takes a cup of wine, gives thanks, and passes the vessel around for all to drink saying, "This cup that is poured out for you is the new covenant in my blood." (Luke 22:19-20) Thus Jesus institutes the Eucharist sacrament most Christian denominations follow today.

PRAYER AND CONFRONTATION IN THE GARDEN

After the Passover meal, Jesus leads his disciples to the Garden of Gethsemane, where most of the men fall asleep. Jesus moves to be by himself and addresses God. Three times he begs his Father to find a way to prevent him from being crucified for the sins of the world, but each prayer concludes with, "[Yet] not what I want, but what you want." (Mark 14:36) After the third request, Jesus accepts his fate and goes to awaken his sleeping disciples.

Suddenly the dark night lights up with torches as his

disciple Judas leads a crowd of armed guards into the garden. To identify Jesus, Judas betrays him by kissing him. When the guards move in, Peter draws a sword and cuts off one man's ear. But Jesus tells him to put his sword away. He then heals the man's ear and submits as they tie him up and lead him to prison.

ACCUSED OF BLASPHEMY

The guards bring Jesus to Caiaphas, who assembles the Jewish council for a hasty trial. Jesus gives the council the proof they need to convict him when he states that he is the Messiah. Caiaphas declares Jesus guilty of blasphemy, and the council pronounces his death sentence. After he is beaten, they take him to Pontius Pilate, the Roman governor.

Pilate listens to the Jewish leaders' accusations against Jesus but is uninterested in their charge of blasphemy. Instead, he focuses on one claim and asks Jesus, "Are you the King of the Jews?" When Jesus says he is and that his kingdom is not of this world, Pilate seems reluctant to pronounce a death sentence. After trying several different alternatives, he gives in to the pressure from the Jews, who want to crucify Jesus, and condemns him to death.

A CRUEL DEATH

Jesus is forced to carry the beam of the cross as he is marched toward a hill called Golgotha. Weakened by the flogging he has received, Jesus falls and is unable to get up, and the soldiers order a nearby man, Simon of Cyrene, to carry the beam the rest of the way.

Jesus's crucifixion begins that Friday morning at nine o'clock. Roman soldiers drive heavy iron spikes through his wrists and heel bones. Then the soldiers raise the cross between two thieves and place a sign above his head that reads "Jesus of Nazareth, the King of the Jews."

Since Jewish tradition required that the dead be buried before Sabbath begins, the rabbis ask the soldiers to break the men's legs to hasten death. But when soldiers come to Jesus, they see he is already dead and pierce his side instead. The Roman centurion in charge of the crucifixion sees how Jesus dies and exclaims, "Truly this man was God's Son!" (Matthew 27:54)

Following the crucifixion, Joseph of Arimathea, a rich man and a believer, asks to take possession of the body and removes it from the cross. He wants to give Jesus a proper burial before the start of the Sabbath. With the help of Nicodemus, a Pharisee who favored Jesus, Joseph wraps Jesus's body in linen along with spices, places it in his own family's plot in a cave, and rolls a large stone in front to seal the tomb.

***The Descent from the Cross* is the central panel in a triptych by an unknown artist. Opposite: *Ascension de Cristo Ante los Discipulos* by an unknown artist.**

JESUS RISES FROM THE GRAVE

Friday evening and Saturday, Jesus's friends and enemies consider the meaning of his death and burial. But on Sunday, all understanding is overturned as an earthquake rattles the land and an angel descends from heaven like a streak of lightning. As told in Matthew, the angel rolls the stone from Jesus's tomb, so frightening the armed guards posted outside that they swoon and faint. When the soldiers revive, they find the tomb empty, rush to tell the Jewish leaders, and are bribed to say Jesus's disciples stole the body.

As this scene unfolds, follower Mary Magdalene makes her way to the tomb with a group of women to bring more spices. Seeing the disarray, she runs to tell Peter and John that Jesus's body is missing. John writes that he and Peter go to the tomb to confirm Mary Magdalene's report. The disciples are both startled to see the burial clothes lying in place.

FINAL WORDS

Jesus speaks only seven times in his six hours on the cross

1. "Father, forgive them; for they do not know what they are doing."(Luke 23:34) Jesus asks God to forgive the soldiers who nail him to the cross.
2. "Truly I tell you, today you will be with me in Paradise." (Luke 23:43) Hanging between two criminals being crucified, Jesus responds to one's request to remember him.
3. "Woman, here is your son." Then he says to the disciple, "Here is your mother." (John 19:26-27) Jesus asks John to take care of Mary.
4. "My God, my God, why have you forsaken me?" (Matthew 27:46) In the final hour of his life, Jesus feels deserted by God.
5. "I am thirsty." (John 19:28) Jesus's only expression of physical suffering.
6. "Father, into your hands I commend my spirit." (Luke 23:46) Jesus cries out as he dies.
7. "It is finished." (John 19:30) In his last words, Jesus knows his earthly mission is accomplished.

JESUS APPEARS TO MARY

John and Peter depart to find the other disciples, while Mary Magdalene lingers outside the tomb weeping. When she sees a man she assumes to be the gardener, she asks him whether he knows where Jesus's body is. She hears the man say, "Mary!" and she immediately knows it is Jesus. As she clings to him, Jesus tells her to spread the word to his disciples.

The disciples, however, are skeptical, according to Luke, and don't believe it when the women say they've seen Jesus alive. Returning from the cave, Peter joins the disciples and says the Lord has also appeared to him. Later that night, the disciples gather in a locked room. Jesus appears in the room and says, "Peace be with you." At first the disciples think Jesus is a ghost, but he encourages them to touch his hands, feet, and side. He eats a piece of fish to further convince them. Finally, the men believe that Jesus has, in fact, risen from the dead.

ASCENDING TO HEAVEN

In the 40 days following his resurrection, Jesus appears to the disciples several times to show that he is alive and to prepare them for his eventual departure.

While the disciples are still in Galilee, Jesus appears to them on a mountain, and they worship him. Then he gives them what is known as the Great Commission: "Go therefore and make disciples of all nations, baptizing them in the name of the Father and of the Son and of the Holy Spirit, and teaching them to obey everything that I have commanded you. And remember, I am with you always, to the end of the age." (Matthew 28:19-20)

Jesus tells them to stay in Jerusalem until they receive power from the Holy Spirit so they will be able to be his witnesses to the ends of the earth. As they watch, Jesus is lifted up and a cloud takes him out of their sight. Two angels appear and tell them some day Jesus will return in the same way.

The Death of Sapphira
by Nicolas Poussin (1652).

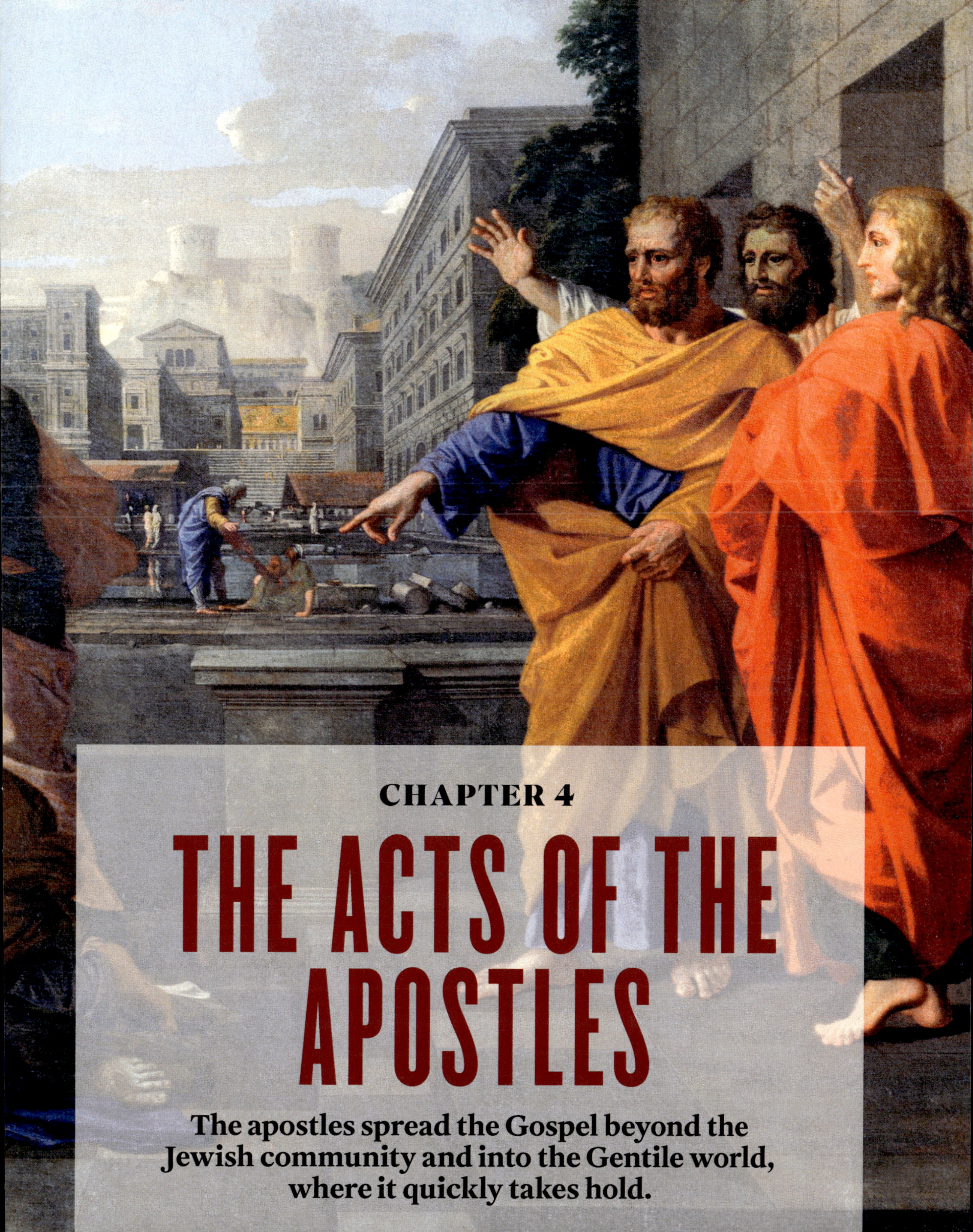

CHAPTER 4

THE ACTS OF THE APOSTLES

The apostles spread the Gospel beyond the Jewish community and into the Gentile world, where it quickly takes hold.

ACTS 1–20

Peter: Leader of the Early Church

The fisherman of Galilee becomes a preacher and healer and opens the doors of Christianity to Gentiles.

Peter is featured in the first 12 chapters of the Acts of the Apostles as he preaches the first Gospel sermon to Jews on the Day of Pentecost. The Day of Pentecost changes everything for the followers of Jesus. They find new courage to preach, teach, and heal in the name of the Son.

TURNING POINT

As leader of the disciples, Peter is often unstable and impulsive. He collapses when Jesus is arrested and vehemently denies even knowing him. But when Peter sees Jesus alive after his death and knows he has been forgiven for his failures, he changes. He becomes a new kind of leader with a unique combination of humility and boldness.

The real turning point for Peter comes on the Day of Pentecost, 50 days after Jesus's death. According to Jesus's instructions, the disciples are waiting in Jerusalem for the promised gift of baptism from the Holy Spirit. Ten days after Jesus's return to heaven, they are praying together with 120 other believers when the sound of a violent wind fills the house. Suddenly, what looks like tongues of fire come to rest on the disciples. Filled with the Holy Spirit, they begin to speak in foreign languages they have never learned.

Jews from around the civilized world have arrived in Jerusalem to celebrate the Day of Pentecost. When the crowd hears the sound of the wind, they gather around the disciples and are astonished because they hear the disciples speaking in their own languages. They are amazed, but some mock the disciples and say they are drunk.

Peter stands up and says, "Indeed, these are not drunk, as you suppose, for it is only nine o'clock in the morning. No, this is what was spoken through the prophet Joel:

'In the last days it will be, God declares, that I will pour out my Spirit upon all flesh, and your sons and your daughters shall prophesy.' " (Acts 2:15)

Peter delivers the first Gospel message, telling the crowd

Juan Bautista Maíno shows the Holy Spirit descending on Mary and the disciples in *The Pentecost* (ca. 1611). Opposite: *Saint Peter Healing the Cripple* by Simone Cantarini, known as il Pesarese (17th century).

that Jesus was sent by God and performed many miracles. He continues, saying that Jesus was put to death on the cross but was raised from the dead by God "and of that all of us are witnesses." (Acts 2:32)

Peter references the Old Testament prophecies to make a point about those who are guilty of crucifying Jesus. When the crowd hears this, they are horrified and call out, "Brothers, what should we do?" Peter tells them to repent and be baptized in the name of Jesus. If they do, their sins will be forgiven and God's Holy Spirit will come to live inside them. Many of them believe, and 3,000 people are baptized that day. And with that act, the Christian church begins.

ANGERING THE AUTHORITIES

Because Peter and the other apostles are determined to preach about Jesus wherever they go, they conflict repeatedly with the authorities. After each episode the penalty worsens, until finally James is martyred in a beheading and Peter's life is endangered.

Giovanni Francesco Guerrieri paints the angel freeing Peter in *St. Peter in Prison* (1610–1620).

HEALING A CRIPPLED BEGGAR

A man lame from birth is being carried into the temple in Jerusalem to beg when he spots Peter and John and asks them for money. Peter says he doesn't have any but he'll give him something better. He declares: "In the name of Jesus Christ of Nazareth, stand up and walk." (Acts 3:6) Suddenly, the man not only walks, he begins leaping around and praising God. When the crowd sees who has been healed, they are amazed and begin to gather around Peter and John.

Peter then tells the people it's in the name of Jesus the man was healed. He reminds them that Jesus was crucified but God raised him up. While he and John are still speaking, the Jewish leaders come up and are angered to hear them preaching about Jesus. The two are arrested and taken into custody.

The next day, the high priest and other Jewish leaders question Peter and John. The leaders threaten them and tell them to stop talking about Jesus. But they reply, "Whether it is right in God's sight to listen to you rather than to God, you must judge; for we cannot keep from speaking about what we have seen and heard." (Acts 4:19-20)

PERFORMING MORE MIRACLES

The men are released by an angel, who tells them to keep preaching. When the high priest sends for the apostles, he is informed by temple police that Peter and John have escaped and are preaching again.

Frustrated, the high priest has the men brought back in and exclaims, "We gave you strict orders not to teach in this name." (Acts 5:28) But Peter and the others say they must obey God, not man. So the high priest has them beaten and then releases them. The apostles leave rejoicing that they have been allowed to suffer for Jesus's sake.

SHARING POSSESSIONS

Luke reports that the group of believers decide to voluntarily sell all of their belongings, pool their money, and live off a common fund. It is a practice that is known among other Jews as well, especially the Essene sect, and expresses a spiritual oneness, so the followers are adhering to cultural norms. Some sell not only their household possessions but also their land and houses and give that money to the apostles, who distribute it to whoever is in need. They also worship together daily in the temple, eat together afterward, and praise God.

ANANIAS AND SAPPHIRA

Acts 5 records the troubling story of how Ananias and his wife, Sapphira, also sell some land they own. But instead of voluntarily donating all the money to the common pool, they keep some of it and pretend they have donated the whole amount. When Ananias stands before Peter to make the donation, Peter says, "Why has Satan filled your heart to lie to the Holy Spirit and to keep back part of the proceeds of the land? . . . You did not lie to us but to God!" (Act 5:3-4) Then Ananias falls to the ground, dead. His body is wrapped up, carried away, and buried.

Sapphira shows up three hours later unaware of what has happened to Ananias. When Peter confronts her with the truth, she too collapses and dies.

ACTS 10

Cornelius: The First Gentile Convert

The earliest followers of Jesus are Jews. Then Peter meets a centurion.

God choreographs a meeting between the apostle Peter and Cornelius, a Roman centurion, two men from very different backgrounds. The encounter will change the course of Christianity as Cornelius becomes the first Gentile, or non-Jewish, follower of Jesus.

• **Day 1, Caesarea, 3:00 p.m.** Cornelius is a very devout man who gives generously to the poor and prays constantly to the God of Israel. One afternoon, he is visited by an angel who tells him, "Your prayers and your alms have ascended as a memorial before God. Now send men to Joppa for a certain Simon who is called Peter." (Acts 10:5) Cornelius calls in three trusted men, tells them everything, and sends them to Joppa.

• **Day 2, Joppa, Noon.** Peter is up on the roof praying when he gets hungry. Falling into a trance, he sees heaven open and the lowering of a large sheet full of animals—some of which are unclean and forbidden under Jewish law. A voice tells him, "Get up, Peter; kill and eat." But Peter protests: "By no means, Lord; for I have never eaten anything that is profane or unclean." The voice replies, "What God has made clean, you must not call profane." (Acts 10:13-15) This happens three times, and the sheet returns to heaven. While Peter is puzzling over the meaning of his vision, the Spirit tells him, "Look, three men are searching for you. Now get up, go down, and go with them without hesitation, for I have sent them." (Acts 10:19-20) Cornelius's three men arrive just then, and Peter invites them in to be his guests.

• **Day 3, from Joppa to Caesarea.** Peter sets out with the three men and six companions from Joppa to begin the 30-mile trip north to Caesarea. They arrive the following day.

• **Day 4, Caesarea.** Cornelius is eagerly anticipating the visit and has filled the house with friends and family. When Peter arrives, Cornelius falls at his feet, but the apostle tells him to stand up since he's just a man too. The apostle states, "You yourselves know that it is unlawful for a Jew to associate with or visit a Gentile; but God has shown me I should not call anyone profane or unclean... Now may I ask why you sent for me?" (Acts 10:28-29) Cornelius tells his story, and the apostle preaches the Gospel to them.

***Peter the Apostle in the House of Cornelius*, a hand-colored woodcut of a 19th-century illustration by an unknown artist.**

While Peter is talking, the Holy Spirit falls on the Gentiles, who begin speaking in tongues and praising God. "Then Peter said, 'Can anyone withhold the water for baptizing these people who have received the Holy Spirit just as we have?' So he orders them to be baptized in the name of Jesus Christ." (Acts 10:47-48)

Cornelius and the Gentiles are baptized, and a new chapter in Christian history begins.

The Lapidation of St. Stephen **by Giorgio Vasari (1573).**

ACTS 6–8

Stephen: Christianity's First Martyr

A believer is stoned to death by an angry mob.

Stephen, a deacon in the new church, distributes food and aid to Christianity's poorer members and counsels forgiveness of sins through Jesus. He is so skillful in expressing his beliefs—many of which contradict Judaism—that the members of some synagogues are offended. One outraged group seeks out false witnesses, pays them to lie about Stephen's teachings, and forces him to defend himself before a council of Jewish elders.

As Stephen ends his speech, he raises his eyes to heaven and claims to see Jesus standing at the right hand of God. Onlookers in the court become so angry they surround the deacon and stone him to death.

VERSES AND INSIGHTS

The origins of stoning and a coded symbol for Jesus Christ

THE DEATH PENALTY
In the 1st century A.D., stoning was an expression of popular wrath, and one of the most common types of capital punishment, along with burning and hanging. The Bible in fact names 18 offenses that are punishable by stoning, including adultery, prostitution, murder, and blasphemy.

VERSE TO KNOW
"Lord, do not hold this sin against them." (Acts 7:60)

IXOYE
The letters IXOYE, from the Greek word for fish, are also an acronym in Greek for Jesus Christ, God's Son, Savior. The letters, drawn inside a fish, were a coded symbol early Christians used to identify themselves. If a Christian met a stranger while traveling, he or she would draw a half a fish in the sand. If the other person completed the drawing, the two knew it was safe to discuss the Lord.

ACTS; ROMANS; 1 AND 2 CORINTHIANS; GALATIANS; EPHESIANS; PHILIPPIANS; COLOSSIANS; 1 AND 2 THESSALONIANS

Paul: A Missionary to Gentiles

A Jew becomes a believer and travels throughout the Roman Empire preaching about the new Christian religion.

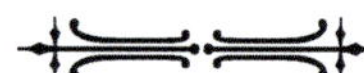

Standing among the crowd of rock throwers, a young Pharisee named Saul holds the coats of those stoning Stephen. Saul, who lives in Jerusalem, is Jewish and known for defending his faith at all cost.

In seeking to protect his faith, Saul searches out and persecutes Jews who follow Christ on grounds that they are blasphemers and should be punished.

A DRAMATIC CONVERSION

Saul embarks on a mission to halt the further spread of Christianity and asks a high priest for letters to the synagogues in Damascus. He plans to travel abroad, arrest believers in the Way, as Christianity is now called, and force them back to Jerusalem.

But as Saul nears Damascus, a bright light appears, shining around him, and he falls to the ground, blinded. "Saul, Saul, why do you persecute me?" a mysterious voice asks. When Saul responds, insisting that the speaker identify himself, he hears these words: "I am Jesus, whom you are persecuting. But get up and go into the city, and you will be told what you must do." (Acts 9:5-6)

Unable to see, Saul is led into Damascus, where he spends three days neither eating nor drinking but only thinking about how wrong he has been about the Way and in persecuting Jesus's followers. He is then met by

In *La Conversion de San Pablo*, an unknown artist depicts Paul falling from a horse. No such horse is mentioned in Acts 9.

Ananias, a disciple of Jesus, who returns Saul's sight by the laying on of hands.

Saul is baptized and within a few days is proclaiming in synagogues that Jesus is the Messiah, the Son of God. From that day on, Saul preaches about Jesus with the same fervor he once used when he persecuted Christians.

SPREADING THE WORD

While Saul and Barnabas, another disciple, are serving Christians in Syria, the Holy Spirit tells church leaders in Antioch to send these men abroad to preach the Gospel. After fasting, praying, and laying hands on Saul and Barnabas, the leaders send the two out to spread the word throughout Galatia.

FIRST STOP: CYPRUS

Saul and Barnabas and a third traveler, John Mark, sail to the island of Cyprus, where Barnabas was raised, to begin their missionary work. In Paphos, the three men meet with the Roman proconsul, Sergius Paulus, who wants to hear their message. A Jewish false prophet named Bar-Jesus interferes and tries to turn Paulus against his visitors.

Saul, who the writer of Acts mentions is "also called Paul" (Acts 13:9), curses Bar-Jesus. "You son of the devil, you enemy of all righteousness, full of all deceit and villainy, will you not stop making crooked the straight paths of the Lord?" he says. "You will be blind for a while, unable to see the sun." (Acts 13:10-11) When Bar-Jesus then loses his sight, the proconsul is so astonished that he accepts the word of Jesus.

ENERGIZING THE CROWDS

For the remainder of Acts and the New Testament, Saul goes by the name Paul. After Paul and Barnabas sail to Perga on the Galatian mainland, John Mark disrupts the trip by returning to Jerusalem, which creates friction between the missionaries. Nevertheless, the men proceed to Antioch in Pisidia, where Paul speaks in a synagogue on the Sabbath and preaches the word of Jesus. His sermon is powerful, and on the following Sabbath, nearly the whole city comes to hear Paul's address. A group of Jews are offended by the challenge to their faith and seek to discredit Paul and Barnabas.

The missionaries are threatened with persecution and leave, but some Jews and many Gentiles who remain in Antioch in Pisidia turn their faith to Jesus.

The pattern of preaching and persecution continues. For three years, Paul and Barnabas travel through the region preaching the Gospel, baptizing converts, and establishing churches. When they finally return to Antioch of Syria, they tell the church leaders everything God has done with them.

A SECOND MISSIONARY JOURNEY

Paul's next missionary journey gets off to a difficult start. He and Barnabas fight about bringing John Mark, who abandoned the first trip. Barnabas and John Mark proceed to Cyprus to preach, while Paul takes Silas and returns to churches from his previous journey.

PAUL'S THIRD MISSIONARY JOURNEY

Paul's next expedition takes him to Ephesus, where he preaches for two years. He is so successful that Luke proclaims that "all the residents of Asia, both Jews and Greeks, heard the word of the Lord." (Acts 19:10)

Eventually, however, rioters rise up against Paul and he leaves for Macedonia, Greece, and, over the objections of the prophets, Jerusalem, to celebrate Passover.

ARRESTED IN JERUSALEM

Paul's deepest ambition has been to go to Rome and preach the Gospel in that great city. After returning from his third missionary journey, his dream finally comes true, though in a circuitous way.

One day while Paul is praying in the temple, Jews from Asia stir up the crowd, which attempts to kill him. A Roman tribune rushes in with his soldiers to quell the

St. Paul in the Areopagus **by Giovanni Ricco (1847). Opposite:** ***St. Paul and St. Barnabas in Listri*** **by Simone Peterzano (16th century).**

commotion and takes Paul captive. Accused by a lawyer for a high priest of being "a ringleader of the sect of the Nazarenes," (Acts 24:5) and of trying to profane the temple, he is held for two years.

Paul defends himself, saying he has committed no offense. He asks to be sent to Caesar in Rome so his case can be heard. Along with other prisoners, Paul is entrusted to Julius, a centurion, and put on a ship for Rome.

SURVIVING A SHIPWRECK

When the ship reaches the town of Fair Havens, Paul warns the centurion that the cargo, the boat, and the lives of all the passengers will be in danger if they continue. Julius chooses to proceed, and soon, violent winds and waves pound the ship, and the crew must throw both cargo and tackle overboard. The tempest rages for nearly two weeks, and the soldiers and their prisoners begin to despair.

Paul hears from an angel that the travelers will be safe, and he encourages everyone to be hopeful. After eating together, they throw the ship's grain overboard to lighten the load. The next morning, the boat is wrecked on rocks off of the island of Malta, but the passengers either swim or float on debris safely to shore.

Once Paul arrives in Rome, he is allowed to stay in his own house and he welcomes everyone who visits. Paul has many opportunities to preach about Jesus, just as he has always wanted.

WRITING TO CONVERTS

Once Paul establishes a church and moves on, he doesn't forget about the new converts. To help them remain faithful to the Lord, he writes letters of encouragement and instruction from many different places and in various situations from approximately 50 A.D. through 67 A.D.

In total, 13 brilliant letters are attributed to Paul. (A few may have been written by others working in his tradition.) They constitute nearly half of the New Testament.

Here is a brief summary of the epistles, or letters, that Paul composed to specific churches:

- **Romans,** written to the church of Rome, is considered Paul's greatest work and is filled with doctrine. It focuses on salvation and how people are justified (made right with God) by faith, not works. It is also the only letter for a church that Paul didn't help start but hoped to visit someday.

Claude Vignon's painting of Paul (ca. 1620).

•**1 and 2 Corinthians** are addressed to the church at Corinth, a cosmopolitan city known for its idolatry and vice. Because there are many problems in this mostly Gentile church, Paul seeks to correct the congregation's misdeeds and beliefs. Chapter 13 in the first letter contains his great teachings about love. The second letter is his most personal, as he declares his love for the people.

•**Galatians** is most likely composed during Paul's first missionary journey. It contains a powerful argument against the Jewish Christians, who insist that Gentile believers live by Jewish law. In Galatians, Paul emphasizes grace and living by the power of the Holy Spirit.

•**Ephesians** (along with Philippians, Colossians, and Philemon) is written during Paul's first Roman imprisonment (60-61 A.D.). To the Christians at Ephesus, Paul declares the glorious mystery about "the church, which is [Christ's] body," with Jesus Christ as the head of the church. (1:22-23)

•**Philippians,** Paul's letter to the believers at Philippi, discusses happiness and unity in Jesus Christ. The letter itself is joyful, as Paul thanks his followers for helping him and reminds them of Christ's great sacrifice as he came to earth to die for them.

•**Colossians** describes to believers in Colossae the person and work of Jesus as the creator, sustainer, and redeemer of mankind and the universe.

•**1 and 2 Thessalonians** are written about six months apart around 51 A.D. to the church in Thessalonica that Paul helps start in only three weeks' time.

The first letter includes encouragement to stand fast and teachings about the second coming of Jesus. Paul writes 2 Thessalonians to comfort the converts as their persecution increases.

THE BIBLE: 50 MOST IMPORTANT PEOPLE

DOTDASH MEREDITH PREMIUM PUBLISHING

EDITORIAL DIRECTOR Kostya Kennedy
CREATIVE DIRECTOR Gary Stewart
DIRECTOR OF PHOTOGRAPHY Christina Lieberman
EDITORIAL OPERATIONS DIRECTOR Jamie Roth Major
MANAGER, EDITORIAL OPERATIONS Gina Scauzillo
EDITOR Eileen Daspin
ART DIRECTOR Ronnie Brandwein-Keats
COPY EDITOR Joseph McCombs (2019 edition)
RESEARCHER Gillian Aldrich (2019 edition), Elizabeth Bland (2022 edition)
PHOTO EDITOR Rachel Hatch (2022 edition)
ASSISTANT PHOTO EDITOR Steph Durante (2019 edition)
PRODUCTION DESIGNER Sandra Jurevics
PREMEDIA TRAFFICKING SUPERVISOR Kayla Story
PREMEDIA IMAGING SPECIALIST Don Atkinson

VICE PRESIDENT & GENERAL MANAGER Jeremy Biloon
VICE PRESIDENT, GROUP EDITORIAL DIRECTOR Stephen Orr
SENIOR DIRECTOR, BRAND MARKETING Jean Kennedy
ASSOCIATE DIRECTOR, BRAND MARKETING Katherine Barnet

SPECIAL THANKS: Gabby Amello, Brad Beatson, Diane M. Pavia

DOTDASH MEREDITH

PRESIDENT, LIFESTYLE Alysia Borsia

2014 EDITION

CREATED BY Contentra Technologies
PROJECT MANAGERS Lynn Perrigo, Sandy Kent
DESIGNER Sandy Kent
PHOTO RESEARCHER Nivisha Sinha
SPECIAL THANKS Phyllis Jelinek, Lisa Slone

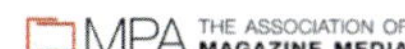

PRINTED IN THE USA

The Flight into Egypt **by Bartolomé Esteban Murillo (ca. 17th century).**

PHOTO CREDITS

COVER DEA/De Agostini/Getty Images **BACK COVER** Bettmann/Getty Images **TITLE PAGE** Private Collection/Johnny Van Haeften Ltd., London/Bridgeman Images **CONTENTS** Cesare Somaini/Electa/Mondadori Portfolio/Hulton Fine Art Collection/Getty Images

IN THE BEGINNING
4-5 Heritage Images/Hulton Archive/Getty Images **6-7** Stourhead, Wiltshire, UK/National Trust Photographic Library/Bridgeman Images **8** Roy Miles Fine Paintings/Bridgeman Images **9** DEA/F. FERRUZZI/De Agostini/Getty Images **10-11** Pascal Deloche/Corbis/Getty Images **13** Lebrecht History/Bridgeman Images **14** DEA/G. Dagli Orti/De Agostini/Getty Images **15** Classic Paintings/Alamy **16** DEA/A. Dagli Orti/De Agostini/Getty Images **17** Universal History Archive/Getty Images **18-19** (from left) 3LH-Fine Art/SuperStock; DEA/V. Pirozzi/De Agostini/Getty Images **20-21** Hulton Archive/Getty Images **22-23** DEA/G. Dagli Orti/De Agostini/Getty Images (2) **24** DEA/De Agostini/Getty Images **25** © Look and Learn/Bridgeman Images **26-27** Pascal Deloche/Corbis/Getty Images **28** Universal History Archive/Getty Images **29** Hulton Archive/Getty Images **30** Pascal Deloche/Corbis/Getty Images **31** Bettmann/Getty Images **32-33** Culture Club/Hulton Archive/Getty Images **34-35** Painting/Alamy

THE NATION OF ISRAEL
36-37 Ann Ronan Pictures/Print Collector/Hulton Fine Art Collection/Getty Images **38-39** Nuova Alfa Editoriale/Electa/Mondadori Portfolio/Hulton Fine Art Collection/Getty Images **40-41** Culture Club/Hulton Archive/Getty Images (2) **42-43** Civica Raccolta Stampe Bertarelli, Milan, Italy/Bridgeman Images **44** Culture Club/Hulton Archive/Getty Images **45** Heritage Images/Hulton Archive/Getty Images **46** DEA/G. Dagli Orti/De Agostini/Getty Images **47** Hulton Archive/Getty Images **48-49** Musee de la Ville de Paris, Musee du Petit-Palais, France/Bridgeman Images **50-51** (from left): DEA/G. Dagli Orti/De Agostini/Getty Images; PHAS/Prisma/UIG/Getty Images **52** DEA/G. Dagli Orti/De Agostini/Getty Images **53** DEA/L. Visconti/De Agostini/Getty Images **54-55** (from top) OEA/F. Gallina/De Agostini/Getty Images; DEA/De Agostini/Getty Images **56** Robert Harding/Alamy **57** Culture Club/Hulton Archive/Getty Images **58** Sergio Anelli/Electa/Mondadori Portfolio/Hulton Fine Art Collection/Getty Images **59** Culture Club/Hulton Archive/Getty Images **60** Fine Art/Corbis Historical/Getty Images **61** Art Collection 2/Alamy **62-63** Eraza Collection/Alamy **64** Francois Langrenee/Getty Images **65** Universal History Archive/Universal Images Group Editorial/Getty Images **66-67** (from left) Bibliotheque des Arts Decoratifs, Paris, France/Bridgeman Images; ZU_09/Getty Images

JESUS AND HIS DISCIPLES
68-69 Tom Grill/Corbis/Getty Images **70** DEA/G. Cigolini/De Agostini/Getty Images **71** DEA/A. Dagli Orti/De Agostini/Getty Images **72** Guido Reni/Getty Images **73-75** The Picture Art Collection/Alamy (2) **76** Mary Evans Picture Library **77** DEA/A. Dagli Orti/De Agostini/Getty Images **78** DEA/L. Visconti/De Agostini/Getty Images **79** DEA/De Agostini/Getty Images **80** Print Collector/Hulton Archive/Getty Images **81** Album/Alamy

THE ACTS OF THE APOSTLES
82-83 De Agostini/Getty Images **84** Sergio Anelli/Electa/Mondadori Portfolio/Hulton Fine Art Collection/Getty Images **85** The Picture Art Collection/Alamy **86-87** Mondadori Portfolio/Getty Images **88** North Wind Picture Archives/Alamy **89** Mondadori Portfolio/Electa/Sergio Anelli/Bridgeman Images **90-91** The Picture Art Collection/Alamy **92** Mondadori Portfolio/Getty Images **93** DEA/A. Dagli Orti/De Agostini/Getty Images **94** Ann Ronan Pictures/Print Collector/Hulton Fine Art Collection/Getty Images **95** Adolfo Bezzi/Electa/Mondadori Portfolio/Getty Images **96** British Library, London/© British Library Board. All Rights Reserved/Bridgeman Images

In the Book of Revelation, John is exiled to the Greek island of Patmos, a fate pictured here in a 1445 work by Jean Fouquet. While John the Apostle is traditionally thought to have authored Revelation, scholars, citing differences in language, debate whether there could be a second contributor. Some call John of Revelation John the seer because of his visions.

Made in the USA
Las Vegas, NV
30 January 2023

66507152R00059